THE LEGEND OF
ZELDA
TEARS OF THE KINGDOM

COMPLETE STRATEGY GUIDE

TABLE OF CONTENTS

GENERAL GUIDES AND TIPS

Unlock more hearts and energy

Life energy in The Legend of Zelda: Tears of the Kingdom is represented as a bar of heart symbols in the top left of the screen.

The number of hearts indicates how much damage Link can take from an enemy before falling over and dying. So the more hearts there are, the longer our hero can stay on his feet in the numerous battles, that much is clear. At the beginning we have to get by with just three hearts and should get the piggy back one or the other. You can read below how to increase the number of hearts and thus increase your health.

The heart symbols in Tears of the Kingdom

Since the very first Zelda part, the hearts as a visualization of the remaining health of Link have been indispensable. You can see them permanently at the upper left edge of the picture:

Depending on the armor you are wearing or how much it has been improved by the Great Fairies, you will suffer more or less damage from enemy attacks.

If all hearts are completely used up, Link dies (unless he has a little fairy in his inventory, she revives him with some hearts on the spot). Replenishing hearts works with the following methods:

- Eat food that you have cooked (found under provisions in the inventory), such as stews, meat skewers, cooked fruit and much more. See Cooking in Zelda: TotK.
- Go to sleep in a bed, such as the Scouting Post, where lodging is free, or a Wayside Stable (where you have to pay for rupees).
- Complete a shrine and exit it will heal you.

Increase hearts and increase life energy

There are several ways to increase the health bar, with only the top two providing permanent improvements:

- Complete shrines to get blessing lights. Exchange four of these lights for a full heart container at a statue of the goddess. It remains permanently.
- Follow the main quest "Investigate the Four Regions" and complete the temples where bosses lurk. A full heart container is awarded for each main boss defeated.
- Cook "Maxi" food using special ingredients such as Maxi Beets or Maxi Truffles. These dishes will increase your health bar past the maximum, but only until it drops below the maximum again.

We see that completing shrines is the fastest way to gain more health hearts in Tears of the Kingdom. Four shrines are quickly found and done. Take the four blessing lights, for example, to the shelter in the lookout post and pray at the statue of the goddess there.

increase stamina

Endurance in The Legend of Zelda: Tears of the Kingdom is a measure of Link's physical fitness.

In the form of a green ring, it visualizes how long Link can, for example, sprint, climb or hover with the parasail before his strength fails him and he has to rest for a moment. Endurance is the second important "value" next to hearts for the energy bar, if you want to call it that. What there is to know about how to increase and regenerate them, we will find out below.

Endurance in Zelda: Tears of the Kingdom

Stamina was already available in a significantly reduced form in Zelda: Skyward Sword and you really know the system from the direct predecessor Breath of the Wild.

Stamina is not permanently visible on screen like Energy Hearts, only when needed. You can recognize them by the prominently placed green stamina circle in the middle of the screen

Stamina is required for the following physical actions:

- Sprint: Hold down the sprint button to make Link run faster. The longer the distance covered in the sprint, the more the endurance circuit suffers.
- Climbing: If you climb a rock face, a house wall, a tower, a tree or something similar, the stamina circle also empties. The higher you want to climb, the more stamina is required.
- Swimming: Endurance is also important when crossing a body of water, at least if you don't use a boat or raft for it. "Real" swimming is exhausting and uses up the green circle accordingly.
- Gliding: As long as Link glides through the air with the Parasail, his stamina decreases. If you want to fly over greater distances, the circle must be enlarged.
- Taming horses: Some horses have to be tamed after mounting them by pressing the L button several times. This process consumes stamina (see Catching, Taming, and Feeding Horses).

Replenish and regenerate stamina in Zelda: Tears of the Kingdom

If your stamina is low, you can refill it with a few taps and continue with whatever is physically demanding for Link (the dishes can be consumed while climbing, swimming or gliding). This is how it works:

- Drink Endurance Medicine: This potion consists of Endurance Horrors and a monster ingredient (the horrors can be found in tall grass if you snip it up while monster ingredients are dropping from monsters, among other things).
- Prepare Endurance Perch: These fish can occasionally be caught in the water. Cook them, either individually (a single bass makes an Stamina Fish Skewer, fills two hearts and a Stamina Circle) or together with other neutral ingredients, such as rice or Hyrule Grass. See Cooking in Zelda: TotK.
- Cook Stamina: These green-capped mushrooms can be found in forests, forest-like areas, near trees, etc. Cooking four of these mushrooms together makes a Stamina Mushroom Skewer (fills four hearts and one Stamina Circle).
- Cook Stamina Tubers: The tubers are another ingredient used to restore stamina. They can be found in areas full of grass.

You can also combine these ingredients, i.e. Stamina + Stamina Perch + Stamina Tuber, which will increase the effect. Go to any stable to cook and use the pan over the campfire. Open the inventory with the ingredients and press X to pick up up to five of them. Close the menu and throw them in the pan.

Permanently increase stamina in Tears of the Kingdom

You can have more than one green stamina circle, increasing the duration of draining actions. However, only the above method is permanent:

- Complete shrines: For completing a shrine, you will receive a blessing light (see shrine locations). Four of these lights can be exchanged with a statue of the goddess for a permanent stamina bonus. The green circle will then gradually expand and you can carry out strenuous actions for longer.
- Cook fitness meals using special ingredients such as fit carrots. This food increases stamina with a yellow circle (which is not tapped until all normal green circles have been used). When the yellow circle is emptied, the stamina bonus is gone and you have to consume a fitness meal again.

Reveal the map and set markers

The map in The Legend of Zelda: Tears of the Kingdom is one of your most important tools for adventuring in Hyrule.

The game world is large, intricate and built vertically. Without a map with scenic details, one is quickly lost and only sees a shadowy representation of the areas on a black background. You can play with it, but you can't see much on it. Fortunately, you can unlock the maps of the individual regions and increase the overview.

The guide reveals what you need to know about uncovering and using the map.

Missing map details in Tears of the Kingdom

It will take a while before you reach the upper world of Hyrule anyway (until the main quest "To Hyrule!"). You end up inside Hyrule and don't see much when you open the map with the minus key. The display should look like this

Black background, no topographical detail, nothing to orientate yourself apart from the yellow quest markers (and custom markers to set).

You must uncover the maps of each region one by one, see the following paragraph.

Reveal and fill in the map in Tears of the Kingdom

To unlock the map details, you must find a mapping tower in each region of the game world, open it, and let it launch you into the air.

Link then soars through the air and scans the terrain below with the Purah Pad, which fills the map section with details of the terrain. You see rivers, mountains, bridges, swamps and everything that can be explored in the area

Most towers require you to find a way to enter them at all. Sometimes there is a tower on a rock plateau with water around it and you have to get to the top. Sometimes he is in an enemy camp. Climbing the towers from the outside like in Breath of the Wild is no longer necessary. You "only" have to open the gate, use the Purah pad behind it and let yourself be shot into the sky from the platform.

New details on the map

An area uncovered using a mapping tower looks like this at first glance

You see the names of significant landscape points, such as mountains, lakes or plains (in the example, Gissa Hill, Kalfen Hill or Snipe Hill). Smaller locations in this area and other points of interest will not be shown until you have discovered them on foot.

The further you zoom into the map display with the right stick, the finer details can be seen. Some locations discovered by Link (especially the smaller ones) are only labeled when you zoom.

Click on an open shrine or tower and you can fast travel or teleport to it from anywhere.

In Zelda: Tears of the Kingdom we distinguish between two types of markers:

pillars of light

- These colored markers can be set when looking through the binoculars (open by pressing the right stick). Aim at a point through the binoculars and press the A button to mark it
- Alternatively, you can open the card, press A at the desired point and place one of the six colored markers from the bottom row in the stamp box (see below).
- Marks points of interest with these light signals, which are then displayed on the world map and minimap at the bottom right. In the actual game world, the pillars are only visible if you look through the binoculars. You can place up to six of them at the same time. The markers will be removed once you reach the location.
- The points of light act as a kind of compass and are permanently visible on the mini-map. You can see at a glance whether you are approaching the desired point or not.

stamp box

- Open the map, press the A button at the desired point and you can select an icon from the stamp box from the top row
- Ten different symbols can be used for identification, such as a sword symbol, a saucepan or a skull (e.g. to mark a heavy enemy):

- You can place up to 300 stamps on the map. They only appear on the minimap when you are nearby (unlike the pillars of light that act as a compass)
- Stamps do not disappear when walking to the marked location. They serve as permanent markers, so to speak, for example for important NPCs that you want to return to again and again.

Unlock and use fast travel

Fast travel in The Legend of Zelda: Tears of the Kingdom is a game mechanic to get from A to B quickly.

The game world is huge and the walking distances are long, even if you cover them on a horse. Fast travel to discovered points on the world map, which you can use to skip entire areas and land directly where you want, makes life easier. Read everything there is to know about fast travel, how to unlock it, when it's locked and how it works in this guide.

Enable fast travel in Zelda: Tears of the Kingdom

Fast travel is not unlocked and usable from the start, so much in advance. It takes a while. You first have to follow the main story, specifically the main quest "The Search for Zelda" or "The Closed Gate".

After completing the first three shrines on Forgotten Sky Island (Uko-uho Shrine, In-iza Shrine, and Gutanbatji Shrine) and Rauru directing you to the fourth shrine (Natjo-yaha Shrine), Fast Travel will be unlocked. Before that it doesn't work.

To do this, open the world map by pressing the minus key. You see such a representation with corresponding points

It is important here that you cannot travel to every point, only to very specific ones. The fast travel points are:

- Shrines you've found and opened (they must actually be open, not just discovered).
- Towers you have opened and activated.
- Underground roots that you have cleaned (see last paragraph).

If you click on such a point with the A button, a message will appear and you can teleport directly there without any disadvantages or preparations.

(Note: Locations like Kakariko or stables are not fast travel points, although you would expect them to be. There is usually a shrine near a village or stable.)

Advantages and peculiarities of fast travel

In general, fast travel in Zelda: Tears of the Kingdom has some advantages and special features:

- You can travel from anywhere this way. There shouldn't be any exceptions where fast travel is disabled.
- As a result, there are no restrictions on where Link must be in order to use fast travel. For example, he can also float in water, ride a horse, float in the air or be in a shrine and still use the function.
- Link can fast travel even in the middle of a fight on the overworld, whether an enemy is firing at you or not. Use this to quickly get away from difficult fights

Fast travel between heaven, overworld and underground

One of the special features of Tears of the Kingdom is the division of the game world into heaven, the upper world and the underground. You can switch through these three levels on the world map with the arrow keys up and down.

Accordingly, fast travel between the upper and lower ground is not a problem as long as you have discovered a suitable point there (shrine, root, tower, etc.).

This is how you get from the kingdom of heaven to the deepest depths of Hyrule in no time at all - and vice versa. And now have fun exploring the game world. It should be a lot smoother with fast travel.

to make a campfire

A campfire in The Legend of Zelda: Tears of the Kingdom has various effects throughout the game.

The topic is first touched on in the Forgotten Sky Island when the task is to find a heat source to reach the Gutanbatji Shrine. Of which the campfire is just one option (there are many more). This section is specifically about how to prepare a campfire, what it is used for and what effects it can have.

Making campfires in Zelda: Tears of the Kingdom

A simple campfire doesn't require much. You need wood and a fire source. If you don't have a bundle of wood in your inventory, chop down a tree with an ax and hit the trunk Anything can be used as a fire source: a flint, a fire fruit, a flaming weapon, the explosion of a thunder flower... Anything that creates or transmits fire can be used to ignite.

Here's a quick step-by-step guide to lighting a campfire with the ingredients you've collected:

- Open the inventory, go to the materials, there to the bundle of wood, press X and then A to pick up one of them.

- If you like, you can also pick up a flint to save time

- Place the bundle of wood (including flint) where the campfire should do its job

- Hit the flint with a metal weapon (not a wooden stick), which will ignite the wood if the two are close enough together. Be careful, the weapon can catch fire if the handle is wooden. Quickly put them away to erase.

- Without Flint, you have other options. For example, activate throw mode (hold R), press the up arrow key, choose a fire fruit and throw it at the wood

- Or shoot a thunder flower at the wood. Aim a little off, as the explosion is very large and will throw the wood backwards a bit

These are just a few of the many ways to make a campfire. You can also find them on your travels, for example in the Hyrule Stables, where they serve as a cooking station with a pan (see Cooking in Zelda: TotK).

Open fireplaces in Hyrule have several purposes that they (can) serve. Here are a few tips on how to use them:

- Campfires provide warmth and can be used in cold regions to keep Link's body temperature within normal limits. Unfortunately, they are not mobile and are therefore tied to one location.
- You can put edible ingredients next to it and roast them, such as apples or mushrooms. They catch fire and shortly thereafter, for example, a Hyrule Mushroom becomes a Roasted Hyrule Mushroom. Although roasted ingredients do not replace fully cooked dishes, they noticeably enhance the effect of the unroasted ingredient
- At the campfires you can wait and let time pass. This does not heal Link (unlike sleeping in a bed).
- Light wooden weapons on the fire and you have a makeshift torch as a light source. Or take an actual torch that lasts longer after being ignited.
- Create an updraft by throwing a Hyrule Pinecone or Chili into the fire. The oils it contains create a buoyancy in which you can open the parasail to be whirled into the air.
- Lures enemies into the fire to weaken them with the flames.

Cooking and preparing potions

Cooking in The Legend of Zelda: Tears of the Kingdom gives you the opportunity to prepare food, potions and medicines for long journeys, which can be very useful in combat and exploration, among others.

When cooking, you can use a total of five ingredients from your backpack and use them to create different dishes with or without effects (the latter only refills your heart bar). Of course you have to have the right ingredients in your backpack. Therefore, it is advisable that when exploring Hyrule, you hunt game or birds, catch fish, collect grass, vegetables and fruit that you find along the way.

Cooking in Zelda: Tears of the Kingdom

Of course, Link needs a decent cooking area, a travel cooking pot from the capsule dispenser or, if necessary, just a simple campfire (see detail page).

You can find cooking places all over the world, for example in the stables with the horse stations. They look like a campfire with a cooking pot on it. A cooking spot that you can always return to is located in the scout's shelter. If you're out and don't want to fast travel to the scout post, you can find a cooking spot by the stables along the way.

Cooking with the campfire

Since you can build a campfire yourself at any time, it's easy to make smaller snacks for quick healing. While campfire-roasted or grilled food doesn't heal hearts very well, it's good for minor injuries.

Zelda in the cinema? The Tears of the Kingdom team is interested

For a campfire you need a bundle of wood, which you get when felling trees, and a flint. If you put both on the ground next to each other and hit the flint with a metal object (sword/axe), a spark goes to the wood and you have a nice flame for roasting and grilling.

Now you have to pick up the food (open inventory > provisions > press the X button and then put up to five ingredients with an A in your hand) that you would like to process. Close the menu and throw the ingredients into the fire (or right next to it, not too far away).

With a little trick you can roast or grill meat, vegetables or fruit on a stick. Use the synthesis for this, take a weapon and the ingredient that you want to roast or grill from the backpack and combine them. This takes more time, but you don't run the risk of burning the food.

Because be careful: if you leave an apple in the fire for too long, for example, it will eventually burn and you will lose it. Therefore, it is best not to throw too much food into the fire at once. This takes a little longer, but you don't lose track of it.

Unfortunately, it is not possible to craft dishes with effects on a simple campfire. For example, if you take a pod of chili, it becomes a roasted chili that does fill up hearts. But the protection from the cold, which the fruit is actually intended for, is not produced.

Prepare dishes on a stove

The best results when cooking are achieved on hotplates that are distributed all over the world.

For example, you have a fixed cooking area in the scouting post, which you can fast travel to at any time in order to conjure up dishes. She is in the shelter at this point

Things to consider when cooking:

- You should not cook fruits or vegetables with insects or monster ingredients, otherwise you will get a Dubious Slush (only heals a few hearts).
- So use ingredients like apples, mushrooms or meat and fish together to cook food. As a rule, this always results in a reasonable court.

Many ingredients also have specific effects. For example, if you hit a stamina in the pot, you get a stamina mushroom skewer, which in turn fills up hearts and stamina. That's only an example. You can prepare many other dishes.

What to watch out for: You should not cook two different effect ingredients, otherwise the effect of the respective ingredient will be lost and you will only get one dish that refills the hearts. So pay attention to the description of the ingredients.

Prepare dishes on a travel cooking area

With a bit of luck, we can pull a travel cooking pot from a capsule dispenser and prepare a meal for consumption on the go.

Unfortunately, there is the disadvantage here that we can only cook one dish with it. The cooking pot disappears by itself after use, which means you should think carefully about what you need beforehand.

There is also no point in putting the cooking pot somewhere in order to use it later, since it will disappear after a while, even if it has not been used. Once you've set up the Traveling Cooker, you can't put it back in your inventory.

If you have already cooked some dishes, a recipe will be created automatically.

This is very convenient, as you only have to click on the desired ingredient in the inventory with the A button and then on "Select recipe". You can now see the dishes that you have conjured up so far with the ingredient and you can take the ingredients with the A button. You don't have to search through the inventory to select the desired components. Link has the stuff in his hand immediately and you can swing the cooking spoon as usual.

Even if you receive dishes from people whose lives you saved during your travels, or if you find medicine in a chest, the recipes will be saved.

If you look at the cooked dishes in the inventory, you can also see the individual ingredients (select the A button on the dish and then "Recipes").

Protection from cold and ice

The Cold Protection in The Legend of Zelda: Tears of the Kingdom is needed to be able to withstand extreme cold or low temperatures and to protect Link from freezing to death.

You will often explore areas with Link, for example mountains, where you urgently need this protection. How come? Because Link takes damage in cold regions if he doesn't use cold protection gear. Here you have various options for creating and using frost or cold protection. The guide explains exactly how this works.

Protection against the cold with Chili in Tears of the Kingdom

First, the screen display to keep an eye on. Look for that thermometer on the right If it slides too far into the left (light blue) area, Link will start to freeze and slowly lose his hearts. We can do something about that.

Of course there is armor with protection against the cold, for example the old winter pants for starters. You can find her on the Forgotten Sky Island at this point next to the Gutanbatji Shrine (which, funnily enough, requires cold protection measures to reach). You will be confronted with the topic for the first time on the Forgotten Sky Island on the way to the Gutanbatji Shrine. You will collect many ingredients on the journeys. This includes chili. And how practical, these bright red pods can also and especially be found in colder areas. They are the simplest form of protection against the cold, as the construct in the pit cave tells you.

In addition to chili, all you need is a hotplate or a travel cooking pot from the capsule dispenser to conjure up a small, useful dish (see Cooking in Zelda: TotK). The following composition applies here:

ingredient	results
1x chili	Cold protection 2:30 minutes
2x chili	Cold protection 5:00 minutes
3x chili	Cold protection 7:30 minutes

With chili and a saucepan, you can let off steam to your heart's content. Prepare the chillies either alone (results in the dish Spicy Bratchilis), which already provides you with the desired protection against the cold, or in combination.

You can combine the chillies with other fruit or vegetables that have no effect.

Strong medicine against cold

You also have the option of producing a medicine that protects you from the cold, i.e. a potion. For this you also need a stove or a travel cooking pot. The ingredients for the medicine consist of:

- 1x Cinderwing or Cinderdragonfly + monster ingredient (e.g. horn)

If you throw all this together in a pot, it will make a small bottle with medicine and the desired protection against the cold (Hot Medicine). The number of dragonflies or emberwings used determines the duration of the cold protection.

Campfire against cold

Of course, a good old campfire also helps to warm up (see details page for more details). Place a bundle of wood and flint on the ground and hit the flint with a metal weapon. The spark jumps over and you have a cozy fire. The problem: A campfire is not transportable. You must either remain there or take a wooden weapon and light it. If you have a torch, use it. If not, an ordinary stick will do (but they burn up quickly).

Protection against fire and fire

Fire protection in The Legend of Zelda: Tears of the Kingdom becomes relevant when you explore regions or caves with fire.

The first time you come into contact with the topic is when you climb the mountain of death in Eldin at the latest, since it is extremely hot there and you cannot progress without appropriate fire protection measures such as medicine or suitable armor. Otherwise Link loses energy in a tour and can even die.

The thermometer, which warns us of cold or heat, also gets out of control in this environment and makes it clear that extreme heat prevails.

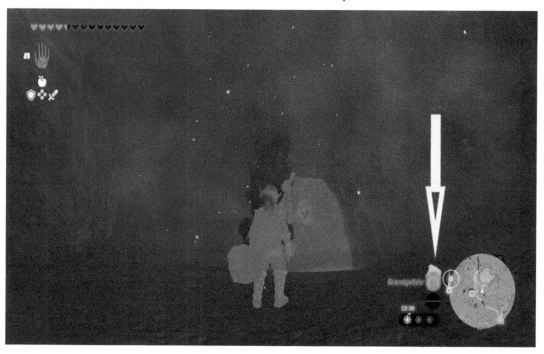

Fire medicine in Zelda: Tears of the Kingdom

It would be good for you if you have already collected some fire lizards or firefighting wings while exploring the game world, as we need them for our fire protection medicine.

Also required to craft the fire-protective medicine is either a cooking stove or a travel cooking pot from the Capsule Dispenser (see Cooking in Zelda: TotK).

You need the following ingredients for the medicine:

- 1x fire lizard or fire wing + monster ingredient (e.g. horn)

The amount of ingredients thrown into the pot by the fire lizard or firefighting wings determines the duration of the fire protection. The more, the longer you can endure in the heat.

Find anti-fire armor in Zelda: Tears of the Kingdom

Of course, there is also special armor for fiery caves that protects you from them once you have put them on. You can buy them in Goronia.

While pursuing the Yunobo of Goronia main quest, you will pass the Yunobau Headquarters. On the left you will see a shop with a seller named Dayto.

The young man only has one item for sale, but it's the one we're after: anti-fire armor.

It costs 700 Rupees, but protects against fire very solidly, at least for a while until you need major protections.

You can also find the Rudania helmet, for example, which also offers fire protection. You get it as part of the side quest "The Treasure of the Lakes of Echsal".

Protection from heat and sun

Protection from heat and sun in The Legend of Zelda: Tears of the Kingdom becomes relevant if you want to explore areas with strong sunlight.

The system comes into play at the latest as part of the main quest "Investigate the four regions" when you make your way to the Gerudo in the desert. Link has several ways to protect himself from the heat emanating from the sun, from simple refreshment to appropriate armor. The guide explains how the heat protection works.

Heat protection in Zelda: Tears of the Kingdom

As with cold protection and fire protection, keep an eye on the thermometer on the display. Once it gets too hot, it falls into the right (orange) area and Link slowly loses hearts

Note that heat protection is not the same as fire protection. The game differentiates again between fiery areas (e.g. in Eldin) and those that are heated by the sun. Anti-fire armor won't do you any good in the sun.

Use water fruits for refreshment

The easiest way to get heat protection in the Gerudo Desert is with an aquatic fruit. Throw them on the ground directly in front of you and Link will get a little refreshment:

Important here: You have to throw the fruit right in front of Link's feet so that when it bursts, it releases water into the environment and Link can benefit from it.

This should only be an emergency solution, because the effect of the water fruit does not last long (depending on the time of day and the strength of the sunlight, sometimes only ten seconds).

As in the real world, it makes a difference whether you are out and about at 6 a.m. or in the blazing midday heat. Adjust your planning accordingly.

If you want to explore wide plains with direct sunlight, do so either very early in the day or very late. Attention: If you are out and about in the desert at night, you do not need any cooling medicine, as the temperatures drop extremely.

At night you even need protection from the cold in the desert, for example strong medicine or other protective measures.

Shade protects against the sun

One simple thing: In the desert, it is best to run where the sun cannot shine directly. Use shelters to catch your breath or traverse canyons that provide shade.

As long as Link is not exposed to direct UV radiation, he will not take any damage.

Cook food against heat

In order to be able to prepare a chilling dish, we first need a hotplate or a travel cooking pot from the capsule dispenser (see Cooking in Zelda: TotK), as ingredients either a frosted melon (found in the Gerudo desert) or a frostling (mushrooms in Hebra) .

Here you have an overview of the composition and which dish is created:

Ingredients	effect
1x Frosted Melon	Cooling cooked fruit (heat protection 2:30 min.)
2x Frosted Melon	Cooling cooked fruit (heat protection 5:00 min.)
3x Frosted Melon	Cooling cooked fruit (heat protection 7:30 min.) etc.
1x Frostling	Cooling Mushroom Skewer (Heat Protection 2:30 min.)
2x Frostling	Cooling Mushroom Skewer (Heat Protection 5:00 min.)
3x Frostling	Cooling mushroom skewer (heat protection 7:30 min.) etc.
1x Frosted Melon + 1x Frostling	Chilled fruit with mushrooms (heat protection 5:00 min.)
1x Frosted Melon + 2x Frostling	Chilled fruit with mushrooms (heat protection 7:30 min.)
2x Frostmelon + 1x Frostling	Chilled fruit with mushrooms (heat protection 7:30 min.), etc.

With the frosted melon and the frostlings you can let your creativity run free when cooking. You can throw the frozen fruit in a pot alone or with other fruits or vegetables that have no effect (eg apples) and prepare various dishes. Each Frostmelon and Frostling used increases Heat Protection by two and a half minutes.

Added ingredients that have no effect usually increase the heat protection by 30 seconds each (there are deviations). As an example: If you throw a Frosted Melon with three apples in a pot, we will get cooling frozen fruit with a duration of four minutes.

Cooling medicine against heat

There is also the possibility of making a medicine that protects against heat, i.e. a potion. You also need a cooking area or a travel cooking pot. The ingredients for a cooling medicine consist of:

- 1x Frostwing or Frostdragonfly + monster ingredient (e.g. horn)

After all the ingredients have landed in the cooking pot, it turns into a small bottle of medicine with the desired cooling protection (cooling medicine). The number of Frost Dragonflies or Frostwings used determines the duration of the Heat Protection.

Clothing and equipment against heat

There is also armor or clothing for heat protection, such as the desert browguard, which can be bought at the desert bazaar. He is in the Gerudo Desert at this point

For 450 Rupees we get a solid sunscreen that should be enough to start with and provides the effects of appropriate medicine or food.

Unlock and use Parasails

The Parasail in The Legend of Zelda: Tears of the Kingdom serves as Link's flying device. "Real" take-off into the air is only possible via detours, which is why it is more of a glider, but many routes can be noticeably shortened and the travel times kept in a pleasant range - as in the predecessor Breath of the Wild. In order to use it, you first have to get the parasail. You can read how this works here, as well as details on how to use the glider.

The Glider in Zelda: Tears of the Kingdom

One of the most burning questions for anyone who has played Breath of the Wild is when will you get the Parasail and be able to glide with it.

It's not unlocked from the start, so you'll need to clear the first stages on the Forgotten Sky Isle and reach the Overworld of Hyrule.

Specifically, it's about the quest "Off to Hyrule!", In which you leave the cloud kingdom and end up in the kingdom. Follow the quest to the lookout post and then the follow-up quest "The Floating Castle".

In it, Purah teaches you how to activate the mapping towers in Tears of the Kingdom. Just before you unlock the tower at the lookout post, Purah hands you the parasail. From now on you can use it to sail through the air.

Use and control paragliders in Tears of the Kingdom

The handling of the sail is very easy. Jump down somewhere (from a ledge, tower, slope, cliff, etc.) and press the jump button again while in the air:

This causes Link to unfurl the sail over his head, allowing him to soar through Hyrule for as long as his stamina lasts. Gliding with the sail drains your green stamina circle, which is why you can't fly around with it indefinitely.

Carry stamina medicine with you and drink it in flight to increase maximum time in the air. If you run out of breath while gliding, Link will close the sail and fall to the ground.

The fall damage can be devastating depending on the height he hits the ground, killing him instantly.

Can you improve the parasail?

No, there are no upgrades to the sail/glider, at least not to improve its performance. However, you can customize the look of the sail in Hateno.

Visit the Balsai Dyeworks and speak to the old cod. He gives you the Sagono Cloth, can cover the sail with other cloths and change it with it (see side quest "Design with Slime").

Gain height with the parasail

With a few simple tips and tricks, the use of the sail can be simplified or optimized. Here are a few special features:

- The sail only works downhill, not uphill, but that should be clear after a few practice sessions.
- Uses thermals to quickly gain altitude. Leap into such an updraft and unfurl the sail, then Link will be thrown into the air and can continue his exploration from above.

- Find a wood-based fire source (campfire, torch stand, etc.) and throw a Hyrule Pinecone into it. The oil it contains causes the fire to blaze up and create such an updraft (does not work in shrines).

- Importantly, the fire source is combustion based. For example, creating an updraft with a flamethrower doesn't work.

Expand inventory and enlarge bags

The inventory in The Legend of Zelda: Tears of the Kingdom includes all items that Link is carrying. An increase in inventory is possible, although this is only necessary for the bags in which weapons, shields and bows are stored. Link can only carry a certain amount of these items, and with the wear and tear of all these items, they won't last forever.

In order to be able to take as much of it with you as possible, you need extended pockets. The guide explains how to enlarge them and carry more weapons, shields and bows.

This increases the capacity of the bags

As in the predecessor Breath of the Wild you have to find and talk to good old Maronus. Maronus is an overly large Krog, a forest spirit who "loves the dance and only shows himself to a few persons".

You will first meet Maronus in the region around the Hyrule Mountains, more specifically on the way to the tower on Mount Tilio. Talk to the frightened Krog and hear his grief.

Before he can tamper with your gear, you'll need to deal with the spooky trees that scare the hell out of him.

Dialogue with him starts the episode "Maronus in Trouble", which only takes a few minutes to complete and may require some Fire Seeds (see detail page).

After the Spooky Trees are burned, speak to Maronus again and you can now give him any Krog Seeds you've collected. In exchange for these seeds, he can...

- ... expand the weapon bag.

- ... expand the bow pocket.

- ... expand the shield pocket.

Each intervention increases the capacity of the corresponding pocket by one place. You can then carry an additional weapon, bow or shield.

The prices for expanding the bags increase as you level them up. We'll start with one Krog per upgrade, no matter which bag, but the numbers quickly add up:

Bag upgrade level	Costs
1	1x Krog Seed
2	2x Krog Seeds
3	3x Krog Seeds
4	5x Krog Seeds
5	8x Krog Seeds
6	12x Krog Seeds

From this simple listing we can see that the prices for the larger bags are increasing rapidly. Since the Krog Seeds have no other purpose in the game, you can bring them to Maronus without hesitation.

Note: After the first upgrades on the bags, our friend moves on. The next time you meet him eg in the Inner Hyrule Lookout Post.

Find, tame, call and register horses

The horses in The Legend of Zelda: Tears of the Kingdom are trusty mounts for Link.

With a horse you can get from A to B quickly and don't have to rely as much on shoemaker's pony. The game world is big and the travel distances are long, so a mount comes at the right time, sometimes literally, after you have found it, tamed it and registered it. In this guide you can read everything you need to know about the horses in Tears of the Kingdom and how to deal with them.

Finding horses in Zelda: Tears of the Kingdom

From the main quest "To Hyrule!", which takes you to the kingdom on the overworld, you can find a horse and tame it for use. They're not exactly being pushed on you.

If you're initially exploring Inner Hyrule, you can look around the map at this point:

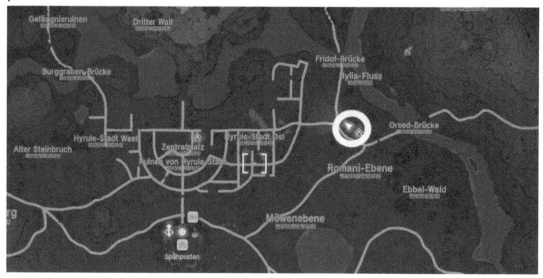

On the northern Romani plain (next to the Ojami'o shrine) some horses frolic in a meadow. If you want to find and tame a horse early on, come to this place and "help" yourself as desired.

From time to time you will also see enemies who ride horses, such as these Bokblins

Shoot the rider with an arrow from the non-existent saddle and you can also use the animal and then bring it to a stable.

The parasail can also be used to catch horses. Hover towards the horse and drop onto your back

Tame horses in Tears of the Kingdom

A wild horse is impetuous by nature, shy and suspicious of strangers who jump on its back and expect a ride from A to B.

When taming the horses, it makes a difference what they look like or how they are colored (you can find out about this in the side quest "A Dream of a Wagon"):

- Spotted Horses: Regarded as relatively easy to care for and trusting. Usually do not have to be tamed after mounting, but can be "used" immediately.
- Non-Spotted Horses: These animals are more stubborn and will usually fight back if Link jumps on their back. They also flee faster and their stats are better.

To tame a horse, you should sneak up on the animals, from behind of course. A sneak medicine can help to minimize the rustling noise when sneaking in tall grass (recipe: 3x worms + 1x slime jelly). Sneak up on the horse until you see the A button to mount it. Link swings onto his back and in the worst case you have to press the L button several times to pat the animal until it calms down and no longer resists. Patting is not necessary in all types of horses. As I said, the dotted animals are very peaceful in most cases and can be controlled directly.

(Note: depending on the nature of the area, even mounting a horse out of the race can work, but this makes a lot of noise, startles the animals and they kick out with their hooves backwards. Ouch!)

Register horses in Tears of the Kingdom

What exactly does registering a horse do? With a registration, which you can do at any barn, the animal is linked with Link as the owner, so to speak, and can no longer "get lost".

First you have to catch or tame a horse. Then find a stable, of which there is one in each region, and take the horse there. In the area surrounding the starting area you can find these three stables, for example

1. Stable of the Swamps
2. stable by the river
3. stable of the plain

(Note: if you want a horse station right in the lookout post, you'll need to complete the side quest "The Unfinished Shelter".)

Ride to the stables and speak to the operator offhand (while Link is on horseback). To do this, you need to press the ZL button to target the operator, then press A to start a conversation.

In the following dialogue he recognizes that you have caught a wild horse. Click on "Register" and you will see a list of the horse's stats and affection. Confirm this and put a fee of 20 Rupees on the table, the horse is officially registered.

Each new registration gives you a stable point (which can be exchanged for prizes in every stable) and the horse receives a stylish saddle and bridle. You can register up to six horses.

What is the registration for?

In addition to the stable points, registration has the decisive advantage that you can pick up and use the horse at any stable, no matter where it is at the moment.

If you have left your horse somewhere, you can recognize it by this symbol. If it's in the middle of nowhere and it's too far to get to it, go to a stable (usually there's a fast travel shrine near a stable).

Click on "Pick up horse" there and it will be teleported to the stable, almost as if by magic.

Use and control horses in Tears of the Kingdom

What should be considered when using horses? Of course, the general button assignment when riding, which is as follows:

button	function
A	Ride and give the spurs. The horse keeps the given pace, no need to use the left stick to accelerate.
left stick	Steer or curb the horse to the left and right by pushing the stick backwards.
L	Pat and soothe the horse when it is acting stubbornly. *
ZL	Targeting, such as addressing or attacking someone from horseback.
ZR	Draw a bow, draw it and fire an arrow.
Y	Use melee weapon from horseback/saddle.
B or X	Jump off the horse.

* Note on patting: With some horses you will notice that they gently defend themselves against your inputs when riding and, for example, break out slightly to the side. In this case, press the L button to pet it. You can tell by a pink cloud around their heads that they like this and are calming down.

Jump over fences and obstacles

There is no jump button for the horse. The horse automatically jumps over low fences and other obstacles as long as they are within the scope of its physical abilities.

It stops in front of big obstacles and shakes itself briefly. You then have to find a way around it manually.

Gallop and top speed

When galloping, pay attention to the number of spurs at the bottom of the picture:

With each press of the A button, the horse accelerates its movement and one of the spurs is used up briefly. If you press the button too many times in a row, the horse will suddenly brake and you will have to gain momentum again after a forced break.

Also, be careful when steering the horses at high speeds. The faster the horse gallops, the more difficult it is to steer or react to changes in direction.

Call horses in Tears of the Kingdom

Calling the horses is a helpful mechanic, but it has limited usability. If you press the down arrow key, Link will whistle a few times in a row.

If your horse is not too far away, it will hear this call and come trotting. However, the system has its limits and pitfalls. On the one hand, opponents also hear the whistles and thus become aware of Link. On the other hand, calling the horse only works within a certain radius.

For example, if Link is in the Hyrule Mountains and the horse is in West Necluda, the call will of course not work and the whistle will not be heard.

Each horse has six stats that can be viewed at each stable (or before registration) when you click Collect Horse:

- Strength
- tempo
- Endurance
- traction
- temperament
- affection

Increase affection by patting or feeding the horse. Open the inventory and take eg an apple or a carrot in your hand (press X > A on the item). Stand next to the horse and it will eat out of your hand.

Find Ramda's Treasure

Ramda's Treasure in The Legend of Zelda: Tears of the Kingdom is a name for a treasure hunt that does not appear in the journal.

You get them from a traveling lady named Sissimo who roams the interior of Hyrule. If you see her walking along one of the travel routes, talk to her and ask what Ramda's treasure is all about. She explains the background and you get three X-shaped markers on the world map (see below).

(Other travelers on the roads of Hyrule also mention King Ramda's treasure. You may get the clue from someone else.)

Read here where Ramda's treasure was found and how to get there.

Find climbing clothing

The marker for this treasure points to a point in the North Hyrule Plains. Maritta's New Stable and Sinaqa-waka Shrine are nearby. Travel southeast from the aforementioned shrine and you'll reach a small cave with a guy named Gladi in front of it.

He's looking for mayois that live in caves and can cling to walls. We've already seen some on the Forgotten Sky Isle.

Gladi also reports of two "somewhat strange people" at the forest stable in Eldin (they can turn in the Mayoi Signa). We can get to the bottom of that later.

Then enter the cave and we'll see what we find.

North Hyrule Plains Cave

In the cave you will meet two nasty robbery slimes. They are only vulnerable at their red core. Approach carefully and watch for the moment when they open their mouths. Strike the red tender spot quickly and they'll be briefly stunned. Use this moment to deal more damage.

Both robber slimes can be defeated in this way with simple melee weapons. Of course you have other options (e.g. combine thunder flowers with arrows and deal explosion damage, etc.).

After the victory you collect the robber slime stone, find a travel two-hander and two chests. One contains a soldier's shield, the other an amber.

After that you have to get to the level above the small waterfalls. This works wonderfully with the ceiling jump. Follow the course of the water and grab some Glowing Cavefish.

A horror blind is crawling around on the wall. Take a picture of him and take him out with arrows. He drops a staff with halberd, an adventurous construction.

Continue up the cave and pay attention to the waterfall at this point (Using the Ultra Hand will help locate the chest)

Behind the waterfall you will find the first part of King Ramda's treasure:

- Climbing Glove: Increases climbing speed and allows effortless climbing without slipping.

Follow the course of the cave until you see a mayoi sticking to the ceiling. Arrow him and collect the signum left behind. This completes the place and you can leave it.

Find lightning protection clothing

The second treasure marker points to a point south of Inner Hyrule. The Tendjiten Shrine is right next to it and is great for fast travel.

At the marked spot you will discover a cave entrance, but it is blocked by rocks. Take a weapon with a boulder on top (you can find a synthesis boulder right next to it in a pinch) and open it.

Cave at Flute Grass Hill

After the first bats have been dealt with, it goes deeper into the cave. Essentially we have two paths. But first shoot the mayoi from the ceiling.

Behind this pile of rocks, which you get rid of in the usual way, are two Electric Batbiters lurking, as well as a few crystals that drop Firestone or Amber:

Continue past those wooden tendrils on the other side. Smash them with a sharp weapon, e.g. a sword:

Drop behind it with the sail and finish off the stalbokblins as they rise (with smacks on their heads once they fall off).

Loot the area and go into the next room. At the top right you can see more brushwood to smash. In the chest behind there is a Soldier's Shield.

On the left side you use the ceiling jump and get into a passage with a robbed slime on the ceiling. Wait for him to spit a rock, hide around the corner and use the time reverse on the rocks. He flies back to the slime, stuns him, and you can deal damage with your bow and arrows (or run and hit; or just run under him).

Behind it you destroy some rocks again and meet an electro-robber slime. The easiest way to fight him with arrows is to dodge his electric missiles and shoot the core as soon as it's exposed. Ideally, combine arrows with slime jelly to increase damage. The slime drops Electro Fruits, an Electro Looty Slime Brick, and a chest.

In the north-eastern part of the room, another rock wall can be destroyed and behind it we discover the second part of King Ramda's treasure:

- Insulating Armor: Rubber armor that provides electrical protection, such as electric shock.

The last marker points to a point at Gongol Hill, which is in Ranelle (northwest of Ranelle Swamp), north-east of Inner Hyrule.

Just cross the Orsed Bridge over the Hylia River next to the Ojami'o Shrine and you're not far from the X-shaped marker.

Cave at Gongol Hill

In the cave you can get a lot of loot. There are many crystals and co. to collect. Place enough glow seeds for better orientation.

In the middle of the cave rises an Iwarok, a small intermediate boss (see detail page) that you can defeat, but you don't have to. Climb onto his back and hit the glowing crystal, that's the short version.

After the Iwarok you can shoot a mayoi from the ceiling and collect its signum. But where is the treasure?

Destroy the ores on the north-east wall and another passage will open up above:

Climb up and follow it to the treasure chest, which means you've already ended the search. Inside is:

- Barbarian Garments: Garments of a warrior tribe that increase the wearer's courage and attack power.

Once all three pieces of clothing have been found, the search for Ramda's treasure is over.

WALKTHROUGH FORGOTTEN SKY ISLAND - ALL KROGS & SHRINES

The Legend of Zelda: Tears of the Kingdom, the sequel to The Legend of Zelda: Breath of the Wild, is an incredibly large game. With our walkthrough for the first area you enter - Forgotten Skyisland - you collect all the Krogs, kill the shrines and find your way around the game right away. If you need further help, we recommend our guide for all shrines in Tears of the Kingdom, the walkthrough for all temples, our locations of all Krogs in the game (everything is constantly updated, but the latter article is of course very time-consuming), the list all fountains with gameplay tips

Now our Forgotten Sky Island walkthrough begins. As soon as you start Tears of the Kingdom, a cutscene begins. Just linearly follow the tasks that the game sets for you. You can not go wrong. Our walkthrough starts with the Uko-uho Shrine. You can't miss that either.

Here you get the essential ability Ultra Hand, with which you connect things together and get a first light of blessing.

You can exchange four of these items for a new heart container or additional stamina. But we'll get to that later.

Uko-uho Shrine

The first obstacle in the shrine is a simple crack in the ground. Take the slab with the Ultra Hand, place it across the gap and run to the other side. There is now a wider gap waiting. Grab both of the plates lying there, stick them together and thus overcome the obstacle.

The third task is already the last one. Here you have to turn the hook and place it in the middle of a wooden board. Connect the parts, hang the self-made gondola on the track and drive over. If your rope platform leaves without you, you can simply run down, grab the vehicle and pull it back up. This was your first shrine - congratulations!

To the In-izu Shrine

You can both see the In-izu Shrine and the Gutanbatji Shrine Shrine with the binoculars. First we go to the appearance on your right. If you look around in the direction of the shrine, you'll see a track going in the desired direction. At the starting point of the rails just around the corner you build another gondola and go down.

Once in the new area, place logs across the gap in the broken bridge to cross it. To your right you can see a floating island with a ruin. You can reach them by using the floating blocks to close the gap.

One of these hover blocks is right next to the island, you can find a few more in the area to your left by the construct that teaches you to hunt. In the chest on the island there is an amber, some apples are also waiting.

If you keep walking, you will see another floating island. Approaching it directly from the west, you will discover more floating blocks. Place them like stair steps and then climb up to get onto the island. You will be rewarded with Sonau energy orbs and arrows.

Enemy constructs await you further towards the shrine. Defeat her to get the contents of her chest, it's an opal. If you look to the west, you will see a small floating island connected by rails. In front of it is a Krog, he wants to go to his friend on the island, but he can hardly move because his backpack is so heavy.

You know how it works: Build a gondola out of logs and a hook. Don't forget to grab the Krog with the Ultra Hand and take it with you on the ride. As thanks, you will receive two Krog Seeds from the reunited couple. Now you can go down one floor in your gondola, where you can continue.

If you forgot the Krog, that's no problem. From the bottom you can simply climb back up the rock face to the start of the rails. And from the island you can even use the sail glued to the gondola to go up the rails again thanks to the wind drive.

Below you fight the sporadic slime enemies and then build a raft out of logs and a sail with the Ultra Hand. On the other side of the bank you will find the In-izu Shrine.

In-izu Shrine

In this shrine you will learn the synthesis with which you stick items to your weapons, shields and arrows to change effects or increase the attack power.

Connect the rusty sword on the ground to one of the boulders. Then hit the broken stone wall several times to reveal the path. In the room after that, demolish the pillar on the left in the same way. On top is a box with arrows. Then turn right and harvest the Fire Fruits. Aim your bow at the end of the room up - there's a crate on a platform. Connect an arrow to the fire fruit, use it to burn the plants around the box and wait for it to fall. Then get the small key from the chest.

Now you come to the last task of the shrine: Defeat the construct opponent. Be careful, he can also use a bow and has a much larger range than normal constructs. After the entrance to this room, there is a slightly elevated level to your right, where you can pick some fire fruits. On the left you will find fire bowls and two weapons if you are blank. If you are victorious, you will receive another blessing and the In-izu Shrine is complete.

To Gutanbatji Shrine

Immediately after you come out of the In-izu Shrine, you will see a cracked spot on the rock face on the right. Smash them and find wooden arrows behind them. Now follow the path and watch slimes fight constructs - use this to your advantage and wait until both parties have decimated themselves. A construct mini camp follows, defeat the two opponents to get an Alpha Warrior Blade in the box.

Your path now leads you into the first cave, the cave by the lake. You smash the glittering pillars with a blunt weapon and get flint. The odd pale frog jumping around here is a mayoi. Kill him to collect his drop, a Mayoi Signum. Inside the box you will find an old toga - better than your current outfit, so put it on right away.

Also look around for a brittle wall in the small cave, behind it are more crystals to destroy, from which you can extract rhodonite and rock salt, among other things. If you put a rhodonite with synthesis on your weapon, it deals fire damage. You can also later sell the gems to merchants for good money.

Back in daylight you can see the fan raft area from the pre-release 10 minute gameplay demo. But first turn right and follow the path. You come to some of the big floating blocks. Use the Ultra Hand to move them so you can get down. There you can already see a waiting construct. It's best to target it from a safe distance, but be careful, it can also shoot arrows. Once it's gone, push the blocks so that you can hop down to the area where the construct was.

Reach the crate on the platform using your Ultra hand. For example, grab one of the floating blocks and pull it over. In the chest you will find amber. If you can't manage to get back over the floating blocks, don't worry, you'd better climb the roots on the side of the small area. At the top of the plateau there are some birds that you can kill to eat and in the middle of the conspicuously large, hollow tree you will find a pile of leaves on the ground. Light it up with a Firefruit Arrow and another Krog will appear underneath, which will give you a Krog Seed. Now jump or climb back down where you came out of the cave.

Now you build the raft with the fan and cross over to the other side. Cook something warm, it's off to the cold. To cook you have to switch to the menu with the plus button, switch to the "Materials" tab and select the individual ingredients with the A button.

Then go to "take it in hand". You can throw up to five ingredients into the pot at the same time. This results in different recipes with different effects on Link. If you just combine chilies together, you'll get fried chilis, which will heal you but also keep you warm for a while.

Once you have climbed the first set of stairs, you should look at the floor. There you will recognize brittle rocks again. Smash them with a blunt heavy weapon. In the cave below you can find some mushrooms and Sonau energy orbs, but also a floating balloon with a target on it where the cave wall is missing. Shoot him down with a bow and arrow and get another Krog Seed.

Climb back up and move forward. A camp with three opponents follows. Defeat them and find an opal in the chest. Continue to the next cave. Glue a fan to the back of the lorry, put it on the track and start driving.

The cave is aptly named Mine Cave. Get out when the cart has hit the obstacle. Combine glow seeds with arrows to place glowing flowers so you can see in the darkness. Or you throw a glow seed, that saves arrows.

Here you will find glittering clusters of crystals again. Destroy them to get the Sonanium resource. At the end of the cave, a construct tells you what to do with it. You can also exchange the metal for energy spheres and energy crystals. The other construct at the exit gives you three capsules with fans. Be sure to take them with you.

Make a fan on the lorry and drive along the rails. You will come to a plateau with several things to do.

On the one hand you can see a large capsule machine here. Here you can exchange Sonau resources for components. You can get fan capsules, travel cooking pot capsules and more there. Each machine is equipped slightly differently. If you put items in the machine that are incompatible, it spits them out again. The more you put into the machine slot at once, the more spheres you get, the conversion is not 1:1.

From the current area you should also see some kind of lighthouse with a red light. There you will find an optional mini-boss. If you want to defeat him, use the ultra hand to push the floating block so that you can hop over to his small island. The Construct Golem awakens when you approach it.

Its weak point is a cube that looks different from the rest. Use arrows and melee attacks on this very cube and the construct will fall to the ground. Gather the loot and glue the leftover synthesised combine-like object to one of your weapons for a hefty damage bonus.

Back on the platform with the capsule machine, you'll find a separated pair of Krogs again. Put a fan on a lorry and drive the Krog over to his buddy, get two seeds again as a reward and open the box. It's tempting now to put the cart on top of the rails that go on.

Resist the temptation and first build a hook on your vehicle. Then hang it on the left rail instead of putting the cart on the rails. There is a gap in the track on the right and you would fall to your death. Once at the top you will find apples, a travel cooking pot capsule in the chest and energy orbs. Jump back to the platform with the capsule machine.

Now turn in the direction of the cave, there it goes on. Inside is a cooking station and in front of it are chili peppers, be sure to take them with you and cook some warming food. Follow the path up in the cave and watch out for the two bats.

Further up, a fork goes back down to the right, take it and kill the mayoi to collect the signum. Below you will find Gems and Glow Seeds. Destroy the crumbling wall and you'll come out again at the fireplace.

Follow the path up into the cave again until you come to light again. Eat a warming meal, if necessary, and turn left first. There you will see a kind of cube. Grab the loose piece with the ultra hand and rotate it to place it in the cube. A Krog will appear and reward you with a Krog Seed. Continue with the Gutanbatji Shrine on the next page! Go back the path and examine the dandelion on the mountain that has the cave exit you came through. Touch the flower and then the flying seed to get another Krog Seed. Now go right along the path. Two constructs are lurking on the left side, there is also a cooking area here, but you have to light it first if you want to use it.

Follow the path and you will reach the Bottomless Cave. Inside you can follow a path to the left across the remaining cobblestones to a chest containing amber. Kill the Mayoi Frog here as well and collect his Drop Mayoi Sign. Watch out for the thunder flowers by the wayside, put them away. A robber slime lurks above. Attack the red pulsing organ as soon as he shows it and defeat the monster, it will drop a box with opal and materials. Further up next to the cave exit is another slime that also drops an opal, you will also find a chest with a flamethrower. Also picks up the flame shield on the ground.

When you come out of the cave, turn left upstairs. The shrine is above you, but the ice prevents you from climbing the high ground. Cuts down trees and glues the trunks together lengthwise. Lean the result against the wall and climb up the wood. A cooking station, a flint and other resources are still waiting in the ruined house. Collect them and go to the third shrine in the area.

In the Gutanbatji Shrine you will learn how to jump from the ceiling. Use it at the end of the room to go upstairs. On the next floor you dive with the ceiling jump first through the left platform on the right side, on top there is a box with a stone axe. Then you take the path through the right platform, but be careful, a construct with a bow is waiting for you at the top. Defeat it and turn right. Destroy the crates on the ground and go into the cavity. With the ceiling jump you get to a chest with a construct bow. Then destroy the two tethers with one of your weapons and use the ceiling jump to climb the now horizontal bridge from below. Now you jump onto the moving platform with the ceiling jump. From there, another jump takes you to the last plateau.

To the Temple of Time

Now it's time to go back. First turn away from the temple and jump through the overhang on the left. Don't forget to consume a warming meal. There's a fireplace in the tree, and in the box you'll finally find some warm pants that you should put on right away.

Further ahead you can see gliders lying on the ground. If you climb the plateau on the right with the ceiling jump, you can use the capsule machine on top. There is also a fire for cooking. Still using the Ultra Hand, slide the floating block under the island ledge next to the plateau to access it with the ceiling jump. There are three glider capsules in the box over there.

If you feed the capsule machine with Sonau items, you will receive capsules with gliders and more. You can sail from the mountain by glider or you can take the footpath, to do this you have to go back to the shrine.

On the footpath you will find, among other things, Krog seeds. If you decide to walk, the route is as follows:

Return to the shrine and follow the path down from there. You will come to a platform with constructs on it. Build a "climbing pole" out of tree trunks again to get to them upstairs. There is also a chest in the ground behind the plateau, take it out with the Ultra hand to get an amber. There is an opal in the box above.

Now follow the path down the waterfall. Arriving at the river with the rafts, there is a ruin with a fireplace on your bank side. Follow the path from there to the end and you will see another Tetris puzzle. Insert the block correctly and you will receive a new Krog seed.

Now cross the river using felled trees and a fan pod. Don't fall into the water, it's so cold you'll freeze to death in no time. Talk to the construct, cook if you want, and make your way up to the waterfall. After a part of the way, turn 180 degrees and look behind you - you will see a kind of tree circle. There you will find axes and further back another plateau with enemy constructs. Be careful, the constructs shoot with ice arrows. Climb the high ground with another log climbing pole construction (great word) and finish off the enemies. As a reward you will receive three fan capsules, ice fruits and chili peppers.

Now take a look at the map and see: you can jump down one level on the left to get to the area with the Temple of Time. If you take this path, look at the map again at the bottom and walk in the direction of the three rectangular ruins below the small lake that are marked there. In the lowest perimeter, half covered by trees, you will meet a strange flower. Follow her to get another Krog Seed. Now it's on to the Temple of Time. On the way there is a platform on the right with a box on it, which you can jump onto. Inside are three glider capsules.

Temple of Time

You simply open the door to the temple by interacting with it. In it you will find the power of time reversal. Use your new power to climb up the water wheel wings - rewind them and let yourself be carried upwards. Then pray at the statue and open the door behind her.

But: You're still too weak - so let's go to the fourth and last shrine. Teleport to the marker near the marked shrine to the Room of Awakening.

room of awakening

You've been here before, but now you have new abilities and can explore the room. Ceiling jump through the ceiling of the ledge on the left and use time reversal to cross the wheels. Follow the passage to arrive at Natjo-yaha Shrine.

The servant construct in the room can build extra batteries, but you still need too many power crystals or sonanium to do so, so come back some time later. Now enter the shrine.

Natjo-yaha Shrine

This is where your time reversal power comes into play. Jump on the raft coming your way and rewind time to arrive at the other end. You do the same again with the raft that drives down the waterfall. Jump back onto solid ground at the top.

On your left is a large gear. Rewind it and let it carry you upstairs to the chest where wooden arrows are hidden. Below the passage is blocked and two pointers rotate above it. Grab one with the ultra hand and cover it with the other, then the gate stays open. Go through and you will receive the fourth blessing light.

Back to the Temple of Time

The brave come back to the Temple of Time with the glider. If you prefer to travel safely, take the teleportation skill you now master. Climb the water wheels again, pray at the statue and treat yourself to the fourth heart container. Now you can open the door. Follow the path and interact with the glowing orb.

Down to Hyrule

Now the world is yours - leave the sky island by diving down from the platform. Manipulate your flight direction so that you land in the water and don't crash on the ground.

Congratulations, you have mastered the first area Forgotten Sky Island. If you forgot something there (would match the name of the area), that's no big deal - you can always return to the area by teleporting.

ALL SHRINES - LOCATION & SOLUTION

All shrines - location & solution

In our walkthrough you will find the solution and the location of all shrines in Zelda: Tears of the Kingdom. We tell you how you get the coveted blessing lights - for mastering a shrine you get one of them, you can exchange four god statues for an additional heart container or more stamina. The shrines also serve as teleport points, making it easier for you to travel. Because TotK is such a huge game, this solution is a work in progress - we're busy tracking down all the shrines and wrapping up the walkthrough for you guys. We provide the location of each shrine, the guide how to solve it and also how to get the chest in the shrine.

Forgotten Sky Island

Uko-uho Shrine
Location: Forgotten Sky Island
Theme: creativity

You must complete all four shrines on the Forgotten Sky Island in order to progress in the game, you can hardly miss them. This is especially true for Uko-uho Shrine, hence no directions.

Take the slab with the ultra hand, place it over the crack in the floor and run over. There is a wider hole waiting there. Glue the two plates together here and overcome the obstacle. The third task is already the last one. You have to turn the hook and place it in the middle of a wooden board. Connect the parts, hang the gondola on the track and drive over.

If your rope platform leaves without you, you can run down, grab the vehicle and pull it up. This was your first shrine and you will receive your first blessing light - congratulations!

In-iza Shrine

Location: Forgotten Sky Island
Theme: combination

You can see the In-iza Shrine with the binoculars to your right after completing the Uko-uho Shrine. In this shrine you will learn the synthesis with which you stick items to your weapons, shields and arrows to change effects or increase the attack power. Connect the rusty sword on the ground to a boulder. Hit the broken stone wall to reveal the path. In the room after that, demolish the pillar on the left. On top is a box with arrows. Then turn right and harvest the Fire Fruits.

Aim your bow at the end of the room up - there's a crate on a platform. Connect an arrow to the fire fruit, burn the plants and wait for the crate to fall. Get the Small Key from the chest. Now you come to the final task of the shrine: Defeat the Construct opponent who also has the Synthesis skill. Beware, he can use a bow and has a larger range than normal constructs. To your right is a slightly elevated level where you can pick fire fruits. On the left you will find fire bowls and two weapons if you are blank. If you are victorious, you will receive another blessing and the In-izu Shrine is complete.

Gutanbatji Shrine

Location: Forgotten Sky Island
Theme: Ascension

You can get to Gutanbatji Shrine by following the marker on the map. In this shrine you learn the ceiling jump. Use it at the end of the room to go upstairs. On the next floor you dive with the ceiling jump first through the left platform on the right side, there is a box. Then you take the path through the right platform. Be careful, there is a construct with a bow waiting at the top.

Defeat it and turn right. Destroy the crates on the ground and go into the cavity. With the ceiling jump you get to a chest with a construct bow. Then destroy the tethers and use the ceiling jump to climb the now horizontal bridge from below.

Then you jump onto the moving platform with the ceiling jump. From there, another jump takes you to the last plateau. Congratulations on your third blessing!

Natjo-yaha Shrine

Location: Forgotten Sky Island
Theme: reversal

The Natjo-yaha Shrine is accessible through the cave where your adventure started. Use the time reversal to get to the hallway towards the shrine. Your time reversal power is also used in the puzzles of this shrine. Jump on the raft coming your way, rewind time to arrive at the other end. You do the same with the raft that descends the waterfall. Jump onto solid ground at the top.

To your left is a large gear. Rewind it and let it carry you upstairs to the chest where wooden arrows are hidden. Below the passage is blocked and two pointers rotate above it. Grab one with the ultra hand and cover it with the other, then the gate stays open. Go through and you will receive the fourth blessing light.

All Shrines - Inner Hyrule

Inner Hyrule is probably the first place where you become familiar with the game and the world in Tears of the Kingdom. With our list, you'll not only find every shrine the land has to offer, you'll also learn how to solve them and bag the chest(s) there. Use the table of contents to jump to the shrine that's giving you trouble, or just go through the list to check off all the trials.

Zepap Shrine

Location: Inner Hyrule
Theme: backwards

The Zepap Shrine cannot be seen from the lookout tower and other high points south of Hyrule Castle, as it is hidden by the walls and surrounding rocks. You can find him by following the road east of Hyrule Castle north. It is on the island and to the left of the hill, near the deep moat. In the first room, a platform moves in a circle. Use the time reversal on the platform and let yourself be carried upwards. In the next room you will see a torch lying on the floor in front of the locked door. Pick it up, take it in your hand and stand on the raft moving across the water.

Light the torch on the candles in the center and use it to ignite the vines on the wall. The wooden platform burns above you and a chest falls down. Take the bow and face the water again.

Jump onto the raft once it's nearby and rewind it with time reversal. Relight your torch as you drive past, activating the candles next to the locked door.

If you fall into the water, you have to wait a while to get dry, otherwise the torch will not catch fire. You can tell from your footprints whether your equipment has dried: if you leave dark marks on the ground, you are too wet.

In the last room, turn right. There is a ball at the top of the ramp. First, put them in the ball switch right next to it on the ground. Then grab the ball again and place it on the ramp. Release the Ultra Hand grip and she will roll into the bottom switch.

In the meantime, run to the locked door. Once it's locked, go through the now open gate. From there you work the time reversal on the ball. It will roll back up and come to rest in the second switch again, allowing you to go through the second door as well. At the top you will receive a new blessing light.

Kjonnisiu Shrine

Location: Inner Hyrule, Ruins of Hyrule City
Topic: Combat Techniques

The construct opponent gives you instructions that you must follow. The first thing you should do is jump to the side and then launch a counterattack. The timing has to be right for this. Next, do the same thing, only jump backwards.

Once you've done that, it's time to parry. Raise the shield at the right moment, then press the A Button. Then comes the charged attack.

If you are successful, you can go through the door, get a Sonanium sword from the chest and get a blessing light.

Zertab-mats Shrine

Location: Inner Hyrule, Hyrule Castle (U1)
Subject: support structure

The shrine is at the back of the castle in the part that hovers far above the ground. If you're in a hurry, run around the castle on the ground until the shrine is directly above you. Then make a balloon - preferably with the automatic B - and let yourself be carried upstairs.

Two normal batteries are enough to get far enough. If you've already upgraded your battery a lot, so will one. Or you can use the Zora skill to swim up waterfalls.

In the first room you pick up the slab from the floor and put it on the two rods on the wall so that you can jump up one floor with the ceiling. In the next room you take the long plate and lean it against the wall on the left, where the passage is above. Now you glue the smaller plate at the top at a right angle so that you can use the ceiling jump again to get on.

In the third room, the crate is waiting on the left. Instead of building a complex structure, you simply take the long plate, lift it as high as you can and drop it. Stand on it, effect the time reversal and you're already at the chest.

Now take the long slab and place it on the floor in front of you so that you are facing the long sides of the slab. Take a smaller board and place it at a 90 degree angle in the middle of the long board on the side opposite you.

Finally, you build the second small plate at a 90 degree angle on top of the other small plate. The long bottom and small top plates should be parallel. Now take the structure and lift it onto the bars on the wall so that the long plate is at the bottom. Now you can reach the exit in two stages with the ceiling jump. For an effort you will receive a blessing light.

Ojami'o Shrine

Location: Inner Hyrule, Romani Plains
Topic: Combat Techniques: Throwing

The construct tells you what you have to do: throw material at him. The tutorial explains how to do this. Two hits are enough and you can pick up your blessing light. That was easy!

Djiosinih Shrine

Location: Inner Hyrule, Plains of Hyrule
Theme: shape puzzle

This shrine is south of the lookout post and below the chasm marked in red on the map. In front of you is a column, next to you is a separate room. There is a piece that you can use as a bridge. Go into the room, rotate the piece to fit through the x-shaped gap with the narrow end toward you, bridging the gap.

In the next area there are rooms to your left and right. Go into the right one first and turn the two connected blocks to slide them through the opening to fit in the middle. Then place them in the gap on the ground so that you can reach the treasure chest at the top. A spurt medicine is waiting for you in the chest.

Now you take the dice and turn them so that they fit through the hole to the left room. This is easiest if you place yourself directly opposite the hole and the stones are between you. Now you have to turn them on the flat side and put them on the steps so that you come up. A blessing light awaits you as a reward.

Ishodgun Shrine

Location: Inner Hyrule, Old Quarry
Topic: wind power

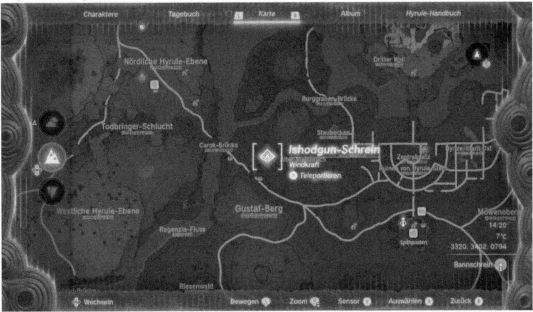

In the first puzzle you only have a fan to climb the hill. Grab the fan with the ultra hand, rotate it so it faces flat, then drop it down the edge from high in the air. Stand on the fan, rewind time and climb down.

Puzzle number two is standard fare: glue the fan to the raft and cross the water. Then you screw the two fans to the bottom of the elevator and activate them. The lift leaves without you, but that doesn't matter: get it back with the time reversal and let it transport you to the top. Thus the shrine is mastered and you receive another blessing light.

Zuzuyaj Shrine

Location: Inner Hyrule, Songbird Meadows
Theme: In motion

First you see three wagons crossing your path. The middle one carries a box. Grab it with the Ultra Hand and stand it across or wedge it in place, then grab the crate and detach it from the wagon. Once it's disconnected, you can put it down and open it. Inside are wooden arrows.

It continues with the construction of a simple vehicle to overcome the roller floor. Turn the plate, on which two wheels are already mounted, upside down and glue the other two tires to the free spots. Place the vehicle the right way up and straight ahead of the hill, stand on it, nudge a wheel, and cross the obstacle.

Now run to the wheel on the right and turn it so that the gate opens. It closes again quickly, but that doesn't matter - run to the gate and turn back the time from there on the wheel, then you can quickly slip through the opening.

The last stage requires you to put a hoop on top of the rails behind the gondola - it has to push it over. Pay attention to the correct direction of travel of the device and that not the tires but the front part are connected to the gondola. As a reward you will receive a new blessing light.

Tendjiten Shrine

Location: Inner Hyrule, Flute Grass Hill
Topic: Combat Techniques: Throwing

This shrine is also a battle shrine. It's all about the throwing here. Kill the Construct enemy with the required attacks and you'll get access to the chest and a Light of Blessing as a reward. Easy!

Tadjiqats Shrine

Location: Inner Hyrule, Flute Grass Hill
Theme: forms in balance

First lay the log diagonally against the wall between two indentations and then run up to the next floor. Here, glue the logs together like a cross and lean the result at an angle into the gap between the platforms so that the cross brace hangs down and stabilizes the other log you are walking up.

Next, lean a single log against the wall and climb up. Now you get four logs to tinker with. Glue three together lengthwise and place the fourth at right angles on top. Then you take the structure and "hook" it to the platform at the top that you want to reach. Climb up the trunks and you are in the last room of the shrine. To get hold of the crate in the water on the left, strap two tree trunks together to form a raft and attach a fan to the right one. Put the raft in the water and let the current near the wall turn you towards the crate. Head over there and get a shield from the crate. Now you move your raft so that you receive the blessing light.

Kamisun Shrine

Location: Inner Hyrule, Forest of Times
Theme: Naked Survival - Elemental

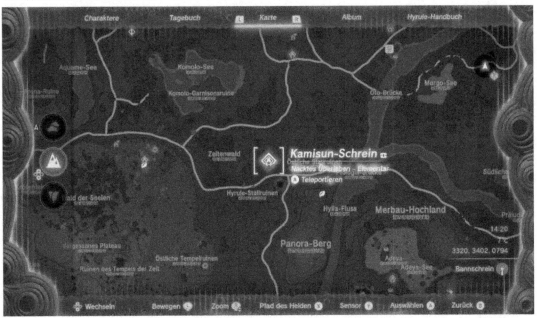

If you enter the shrine, you lose all your equipment for this duration. Everything you are allowed to equip can be found in the shrine. But you keep your skills. Now face the fight against the constructs and put your skills to the test. Using Synthesis, strap the Spiked Orb onto one of the weapons you currently own and defeat the enemies. Destroy the crumbling platform the archer is standing on with your heavy weapon. After your victory, you will receive a shield in the chest in the now opened room and a blessing light.

Location: Inner Hyrule, Gongol Hills
Theme: Springform

The shrine is shielded from view by a gigantic, hollow tree trunk. In the first room there is a steep ramp on the left, on the right there is a switch and a kind of metal basket behind a deep gorge. Take the metal plate on the ground and put it over the gap so that there is a jump for the ball. The ball rolls down the ramp as soon as you press the switch.

In the next room you first glue the plates together to put them over the gap so that you come to the chest on the right. Take the shield and then face the ramp. Take the smaller plate and stand it upright. Then you glue the longer plate to it at an angle to build a ramp again and direct the ball into the basket. After that, the blessing light is already yours.

Kjoqugoni Shrine / Cave at Forgotten Plateau

Location: Inner Hyrule, Plains of Hyrule, Forgotten Plateau
Theme: heaven and earth

South between Lake Aquame and Lake Komolo, three roads meet in an inverted T-shape. There on the slope of the Forgotten Plateau you will find the cave at the Forgotten Plateau. You need blunt weapons to destroy the rubble at the entrance. After that you will come to a room with two horror blinds. Once you've defeated them, look out for crumbly blue stones on the right cave wall. Smash it and kill the Mayoi waiting behind it to collect the Mayoi Sign. Between you and the shrine is another broken wall at the end of the passage down. The stones are not only more resistant, there are also many, but after that you finally arrive at the shrine.

The theme of the shrine is also a clue for the solution. In the large room that follows are ten push buttons that can accommodate balls. However, there are only four balls. To see which switches to put them in, look up at the ceiling - the green circles point to the correct sockets. Use the orbs and go into the next room to pick up your blessing light.

On the right side of the room you can see another chest behind a lattice. To open the crate, take the orb that's next to it and place it on the one base plate with your ultra hand, which you can use to interact with the orb in hand. Lift the plate and place the ball in the now exposed switch. The box is yours and the shrine mastered.

Location: Inner Hyrule, Plains of Hyrule
Topic: hot air

You can't miss this shrine, it's right next to Maritta's new stable on the westbound road. On the right you can see a balloon trapped under a ledge. Take one of the boards on the left where there are more balloons, grab one of the candles around and place it in the middle of the board. Then take the balloon, mount it over the light and let yourself be carried upstairs.

When you get to the top you will see an orange switch above the locked door. To activate it with the balloon, take one of the candles around, connect it to the balloon below and put the result under the switch. The balloon floats up and you can continue walking.

The next room is very large and has several levels. To open the gate to the room with the blessing light, you just have to move a small orb from the ground up. If you also want to open the right room to reach the chest there, you also have to bring the big ball up. There's an opal in the chest - you'll have to decide if it's worth it, but basically getting the key orbs up is very simple.

Grab one of the candles standing around and put it on the small ball, then connect the candle to the balloon and the cargo will float upwards. The ladder on the left takes you to the ceiling. Simply grab the balloon with the ultra hand and guide it to blocked passageways. Pick up the ball and let it roll into the hole or use it.

The same principle applies to the heavy orb, except that you have to use the more powerful flamethrowers to have enough buoyancy. So stick one of the flamethrowers standing around on the ball, put the balloon on it and everything floats upwards. Use the jump in the ceiling in the dent or the ladder to get up there as well and take the orb.

Runa-kita Shrine

Location: Inner Hyrule, Hyrule Mountains
Topic: mode of transport

The shrine is located between Tilio Slope and the chasm marked on the map to the west of it. Just fly the glider west from the mapping tower and you'll see it from the air. If you enter it, you will find yourself in a huge room.

First slide straight across the gorge in the direction of the ball. Grab it and put it on the rails so it rolls down. Before you put it on the next rail, you tinker the two pipes that are on the ground there on the left and right of the ball. That way it won't fall through the gap - it's wider now.

At the next station you can optionally reach a chest. To do this, you first take one of the roof-shaped parts and place one of the three plates on top.

Now place the sphere on the back of the roof shape and the structure between the rails in front of the crate.

Now place the other two on the already placed flat plate to form a bridge.

Now you can jump on it and reach the ladder. The whole thing is a little fiddly, if you don't need a new bow anyway, you can save yourself the chest.

In order to bring the ball to the actual target, you take a roof shape and place it on the ground like a roof. Now place the ball as centrally as possible on top.

However, the shape of the roof is not symmetrical - one side is shorter than the other. Either you balance it out exactly and let your roof-ball construction slide elegantly down on the rail, or you build the flat plates on both sides of the roof shape to shift the center of gravity and to stabilize the construction .

If you have successfully transported the ball over there, sail there with the glider and place it in the hole. The door will open and you will receive another blessing light.

Maqru'kiza Shrine

Location: Inner Hyrule, Hyrule Mountains
Topic: Combat techniques: bow and arrow

You can find the shrine southwest of Rhoam Mountain. It is relatively easy to see from above. In it you will again encounter a combat challenge with a construct that gives you tasks. You use a bow and arrow as your weapon.

The first trial simply requires you to land a headshot on the opponent. The second and last part of the task in the shrine is to kill the three constructs that appear with headshots.

If you need distance, use the ceiling jump on the back of the two columns on the left and right of the room. When you finish collecting the resources, you will receive a blessing light and access to a chest as a reward.

Ekotsi'u Shrine

Location: Inner Hyrule, Hyrule Forest
Theme: fall and rise

The shrine is right by the Forest Stables east of Hyrule Castle. In the first room, stand on the switch, then on the block and use time reversal to get across.

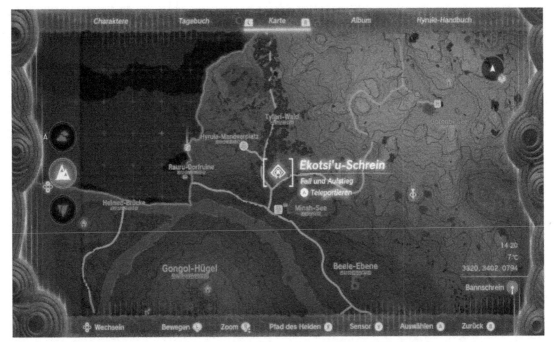

Then you take the block, put it on the right at the edge of the water and get over to the crate. Pick up the block again, hold it up with the Ultra hand, drop it, step on it and time-reverse it to get up. Place the block on the bump mechanism on the ground and press the switch. Finally, stand on the block, time-reverse it, and slide over to collect the blessing light.

Zon'apano Shrine

Location: Inner Hyrule, Hyrule Mountains
Topic: Missing path

The shrine is located on the eastern slope of Satori Mountain. In the first room you use the ceiling jump. When you get to the top, take the block on the right to the left, where a box is embedded in the wall.

Push the block on rails on the floor to the right to the crate and stick the block you took from the right to the other on the left so you can stand underneath and jump through with the ceiling jump. Open the box and take the loose block with you. Stand on the platform above you and jump through to get to the next room.

Once there, remove the metal block below the ledge and place it in the water under the platform above that leads to the exit. Then jump through the ceiling at the ledge, sail onto the metal block and use the ceiling jump again to reach the blessing light.

Location: Inner Hyrule, Plains of Hyrule
Theme: Good leadership

On a rise below the Plains stable stands the Tsutsu-um Shrine. Once inside, you first take the nail stuck in the up and down moving column.

Take the nail, put a plate on it and stick both to the other side of the pillar. You can stand on it and be transported over there. You can get to the crate by simply attaching the nail plate to the top of the crate platform. Use the ceiling jump and the arrows in it are yours. Now you come to the ball track area of the shrine. Now take the plate with the nail on it, which is still on the ground. Observe where the ball bounces off the wall and use the plate with the nail at an angle so that the ball is directed towards the spinning wheel.

This rewinds her with the time reversal so that the ball is sent to the right. Remove the interfering nails in the wall so the ball lands in the rail below and falls into the switch. If you don't have enough momentum, simply insert a nail into the spinning disk behind the ball and it slides into the switch. The next blessing light beckons as a reward.

Riogok Shrine

Location: Inner Hyrule, Plains of Hyrule, Forgotten Plateau
Topic: power transmission

The shrine is nestled between cliffs west of Toadpond on the Plains of Hyrule. You can see it best from the air. Glue the tube to the two smaller gears so that everything is connected. Now activate the switch in the form of a small pillar by hitting it, and the gears will start moving, the gate will open.

In the next room there is another pipe lying on the floor. Glue it to the broken switch on the floor and flip it to open the lattice door. Behind it you will find another pipe. You put that on the lower platform on the wall with the gear so that the smaller platform is above the pipe. Now grab the second pipe and place it on the lower, longer platform on the left, so that the longer tooth of the gearwheel engages and pushes the platform up. Now jump onto the lower platform with the ceiling jump, then onto the smaller one above it and let yourself be driven up to the exit. As a reward you will receive a blessing light.

If you want to open the treasure chest in the shrine, simply put the two pipes on top of each other and "fish" for the chest. Connect the pipe to the chest and bring it down. A construct bow awaits you inside.

Location: Inner Hyrule, Plains of Hyrule, Forgotten Plateau
Theme: Fire and Water

Go to the source of the river of death in the mountains. Once past the spring and standing on the slope south of the river, look down and look for solid ground at the edge. Slide down and face towards the waterfall. Be careful, there is an ice robbery slime lurking here.

Continue to the waterfall and you will discover a cave, the Dead River Waterfall Cave. On the way you get behind the waterfall and into a room with a small pool on the floor. There's a Mayoi sitting on the ceiling here, kill him to get a Mayoi Sign. Now you have to defeat a normal slime and you can attack the Tadarok-un Shrine.

Right at the beginning you take the stone cuboid and place it in the water, ideally with the corner pointing towards you. Now you can walk across without making contact with the water that is under storm. Take the iron block straight into the room after that. Directly in front of you is an iron block in the water that is electrified.

Get the ball out and hang it over the yellow pillar so the water doesn't shock you anymore. Now take the iron block out of the water and use it to block the flamethrowers on the left so that the block of ice reaches the ground unharmed. Take it and put it on the platform with the crate so you can go up and open it. Inside you will find a strong shield.

Now turn to the lava and pick up an iron block - or two. Put them in the lava and cross them. If you only take one block, you need a run-up, the jumps are quite far. Now save the wooden box that falls into the flamethrowers from above and extinguish it in the pool on the left.

Take her across the lava. Now place the iron block in the middle of the water that just contained the ball and build the other iron block on the platform at the top left close to the flamethrower. Now place the block of ice to the top right. Jump through the ceiling from the metal platform, place the ice block on top of the metal block in front of the flamethrower and connect the two.

Now it's going down again; grab the crate and place it on the right side of the platform. Now the box comes on top of your tower and you put everything in the middle so that the metal plate is in the water directly below.

Use the ceiling jump to jump through all three blocks and you will reach the exit of the temple, the blessing light is yours. By the way, it doesn't matter whether you use the ice or the wooden box as the second building block - the only important thing is that the lower part is made of metal so that the flamethrowers don't damage your structure.

Uzas-um Shrine / Cave under Satori Mountain

Location: Inner Hyrule, Hyrule Mountains, Satori Mountain
Theme: Raurus blessing

You can find the shrine - at least a part of it - in the north of the Dalith forest at the end of the large meadow. You have to activate it by getting the corresponding crystal. The ray of light shows you the way. Run over to the cave under Satori Mountain. As you can see, the beam of light is moving - so something is carrying the crystal around.

The cave consists of a circular corridor, so it doesn't matter in which direction you walk. In the middle of the longer path you should look up at the wall, there you will find a chest with 100 rubies. Also pay attention to the rocks above you on the outside of the passage: In a bulge, slightly elevated, there is not only a mayoi waiting for you, which you can kill to get a mayoi sign, but also ore deposits. Don't miss the maxi truffle in the corner either. Now you can face the battle against the Hinox to wrest the crystal from him.

The easiest way to do this is to stay on the hill where the mayoi was sitting. The Hinox can only throw stones at you, which you send back to the sender with the time reversal. Takes a while, but that's how the monster goes on the boards and you don't waste weapon durability and arrows. Now carry the crystal to the shrine.

The shrine requires no battles from you and no puzzles - Raurus blessing means you get a reward just like that. Top! Open the chest before picking up the blessing light and you're done.

Mayan Tsino'u Shrine

Location: Inner Hyrule, Plains of Hyrule
Topic: problem fix

The shrine is right by the Old Transfer Point in Windflower Meadows. Let yourself be carried over by the rotating platform and then press the switch on the ground. A target will appear on the right.

Now go down and insert the two nails left and right into the strange device on the ground. You fix the two tubes to the nails, creating a kind of turnstile. Now run back to the switch on the ground and hit the pillar switch to the right of it.

With the correct timing - let the ball come to a standstill at the turnstile - you hurl the ball at the target and open the room where you receive the blessing light.

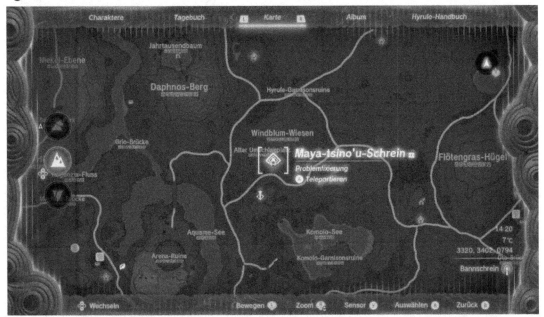

If you want to open the box on the right behind the locked door, you have to go down again. Behind the hanging plate on the right is another nail. Take it and get the pipe taped to the right side of the turnstile as you face it from the counter. Glue the pipe flat to the front of the hanging obstacle and the nail to it, digging into the platform the whole thing is hanging from. Then use the Ultra Hand to move the hanging plate up and rotate it if necessary to drive the nail into the stone, clearing and fixing the obstacle.

Now you wait until the ball has rolled to the last mark on the ground to the turnstile, activate the switch and shoot it at the target. As a reward, you will receive Stamina Medicine from the chest.

Kiujoj-u Shrine

Location: Inner Hyrule, Hyrule Forest, Sorbo Plains
Theme: playing with fire

The shrine is north of the road that goes around Maritta Hill and northeast of the Sorbo Plains. In the first room you can see active flamethrowers on the right and a block of ice on the left. By the locked gate, also on the left, you can see a small switch in an indentation. Take the block of ice with the ultra hand and briefly hold it in the fire to melt it down to the right size. Then place it on the switch to open the door. Go through the door, but take the block of ice with you (the door will stay open). To your left is an indentation with a chest. Place the ice block on the first step and use the ceiling jump to get to it. Then climb onto the block and from there to the chest. Then use the updraft to sail to the platform at the end of the room. Blocks of ice are constantly falling into flamethrowers and melting. Wait until a block of ice just falls out of the hole and stop the time with your time reversal skill. Then immediately grab it with the Ultra Hand and place it safely next to you. Or you cover the flamethrowers with the plate leaning against the wall and then grab it. Either way: If the block of ice is safe, grab this plate that is leaning against the wall on the right. Glue them to the top of the ice block so you can still climb it. Place the block of ice on top of the spiked slide so that it slides down but you can still jump up quickly.

Once you have reached the bottom with your block of ice, you should check again whether the plate above the ice really covers the block of ice everywhere. Take the block with the plate cover and put it right under the flamethrowers from the beginning - the whole platform is one giant switch. Now the way to the sanctum of the shrine is open and you will receive a light of blessing.

The next page continues with the shrines in the frigid region of Hebra in northwest Hyrule. By the way, did you know that the roots in the Hyrule Abyss are exactly where the shrines are in the overworld? This way you can deduce in which direction the next roots should be. And if you find a root underground but don't see a shrine on the overworld map, you'll know where to look.

All shrines - Hebra

Dress warmly to explore Hyrule's frigid Hebra region. You can read about how to get all the clothes and equipment in this solution from us. Also, don't forget to cook supplies to keep you warm. We also have the right help and a guide ready for this. But now we start our shrine tour in the cold northwest. Jump to the shrine that's giving you trouble as usual, or go through the list to check everything. We're updating the shrines as soon as we can to bring you the walkthrough as soon as possible.

Mayan usi'u shrine

Location: Hebra, Tabanta Borderlands, Kukudja Gorge, Forgotten Temple
Topic: power of combination

You will inevitably find this shrine if you follow the quest "The Tears of the Dragon" with Impa. At the northern end of the Kukudja Gorge is the Forgotten

Temple. Go deeper into it and at the end climb up what appears to be a dead end and you will see Impa and the shrine. In keeping with the shrine theme, you'll need to recreate shapes using the Ultra Hand by rotating and fitting the pieces. Place the two pieces against the rest of the right frame to create an identical shape to the one on the left. After that, a construct opponent stands in your way. Defeat him any way you want, strap a barrel to your weapon - it doesn't matter how you do it. In the room after that you have to complete another form. But for now, put another piece on top of the incomplete form so you can get up high enough to jump and slide to the chest on the platform.

Once that's done, you build the form from the three parts. It's difficult to give precise instructions here, but here's a little help: If the template shape is in your back, the rightmost piece goes on the left side of your cube, then the leftmost piece on the ground follows, and on the right side comes the middle part. Remember to rotate the pieces as well. If you have mastered this, you will receive the blessing light.

Orotsi-um Shrine

Found: Hebra, Hebra Mountains, South Tabanta Snowfield
Topic: Courage to fall

The shrine is right next to the Snowlands Stable. First open the big gates in front of you with the ultra hand. Inside you see lasers. Run left and defeat the construct.

Jump up further ahead with the ceiling jump, now take the ladder and crawl through the gap on the right. Jump down to the construct and defeat it. Around the corner is another opponent, he protects a chest, which of course you open.

Now open the small gate with the ultra hand, which is at the bottom of the stairs. Crouch under the lasers and defeat the two constructs. You can only open the green door with a small key. Turn to the lasers on the door. Touch her and drop down. Here you have to dodge other lasers, then you reach a chest with the required key.

Jump through the ceiling and go to the locked room. Grab the ball and let the elevator carry you to the left or right to the top. Put the ball in the switch to open the room with the glider. Take it out, place the orb on it and sail down to the switch that will open the path to the blessing light.

Oshosan-u Shrine

Location: Hebra, Hebra Mountains, North Tabanta Snowfield
Topic: target search

To the northeast of the Tabanta Snowfield and west of the strange square on the map you'll find the shrine. You can reach the shrine quite easily from above, for example from the sky islands. Glue the tree trunk across to the block on the rail.

Add the rocket and activate it so that everything goes towards the target and the door opens.

In the next room, take the long log and clamp it to the platform on the left so you can climb up and open the crate. Then you put him on the wheel by the target and clamp the rocket to it. Activate it and the next door will open, behind which you will get the blessing light.

Mayan otaki shrine

Found: Hebra, Hebra Mountains, Northern Irregular Castle
Theme: Raurus blessing

The shrine is located in the Irrschloss and is not so easy to reach - actually you should follow the trail of pine cones left by a researcher.

The direct way is as follows: Get to the Irrschloss roof somehow. Climb or slide or use a balloon.

Run from the eastern tip towards the center and look into the deep passage canyons. At one point you see an orange light illuminating a corridor. Drop down right there, enter the path in the wall and follow the stairs up.

At the shrine, you must first clear the entrance of ice by lighting a fire. Now you can enter the shrine; since the path was already enough puzzle, you get chest and blessing light just like that.

Orom-waka Shrine

Location: Hebra, Tabanta Frontier
Theme: Rapid rise

The shrine is located at the northernmost tip of Lake Adebar among thorns. Glide to the entrance to avoid getting hurt, or torch the plants if the weather permits. In the first room, take a rocket from the right and place it in the groove of the sloping plates facing the target. Activate it and the door will open once the missile hits the target. In the next room, a mine cart is waiting on a steep rail. Put a rocket on the cart and drive up the steep incline. Once at the top, look to your right and up - there's a crate on a platform near the ceiling. Take a minecart, stick rockets to the left and right, pointing up, and activate them. You climb up and when you get to the top you can quickly jump from the ceiling to pull a rhodonite out of the chest. Now place a lorry on the sloping platform in one of the grooves and strap on two rockets. Get in, activate the rockets and let yourself be carried over. You've already earned a new blessing light.

Iqatak Shrine / Gissa Crater Cave / Gissa Crater Shrine

Location: Hebra, Tabanta Frontier
Theme: Raurus blessing

The crystal you are looking for is in the cave next to the shrine. It is best if you complete the task if you have balloon capsules. Strap the balloon and flamethrower to the crystal and launch it upwards. Then quickly jump through the ceiling and grab the balloon before the batteries run out and everything crashes again.

Bring the crystal to the shrine and you will receive a box and a blessing light without having to complete another task. In the cave with the crystal you will still find chunks of ore, robbed slime and skeleton opponents.

Gata Kiza Shrine

Location: Hebra, Tabanta Frontier, Orni Village
Theme: Riding the wind

The shrine is right in the village of the Orni, you can hardly miss it. For now, slide over to the first platform. Here is a gigantic fan behind you. Use the wind to dodge the laser beams with the glider and land on the other side. Drop through the gap in the floor and destroy the ice by jumping on it. As you hop through the ice opening, keep an eye out for Construct enemies. One of them is on a platform where you can also find the crate in this dungeon. Then you look for the passage with bars on the wall that leads upstairs. Let yourself be blown up and you will receive a blessing light.

Zahirowa Shrine

Location: Hebra, Hebra Mountains, Kassula Mountain
Thread: Dodge carefully

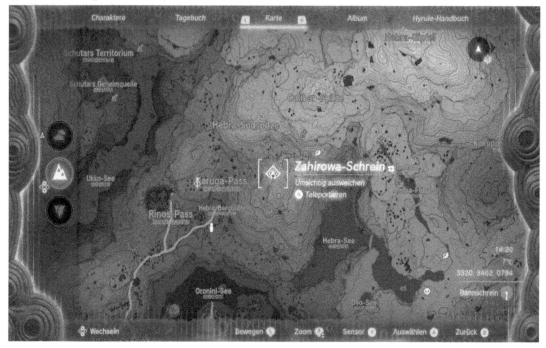

The shrine is located on the slope of Kassula Mountain very close to the tower at Karuga Pass and is easily visible and accessible from the air. In the first room, make a running jump over the laser barrier and then go around the corner.

For the next few lasers, jump over the first, crouch under the next four, and then jump over the three beams side by side from the stairs. Now use the ceiling jump on the moving platform.

Then turn right. Behind the laser barrier are two iron blocks and a grate blocking the way to the chest. Place a block to block the laser beam, but don't stand on the trapdoor directly in front of it. Now the way to the box is free. Get the content.

Now continue down the long corridor. Here a total of three laser barriers come towards you. Jump over the first one, duck under the second one and at the end of the laser grate you stand at the back - the laser doesn't get that far - and wait for the frame to move away from you. Then you run after it and climb it using the ceiling jump. Now you're done and you can grab the blessing light.

Rutafu-um Shrine / Northwest Cave of the Hebra Mountains

Locality: Hebra, Hebra Mountains
Theme: Raurus blessing

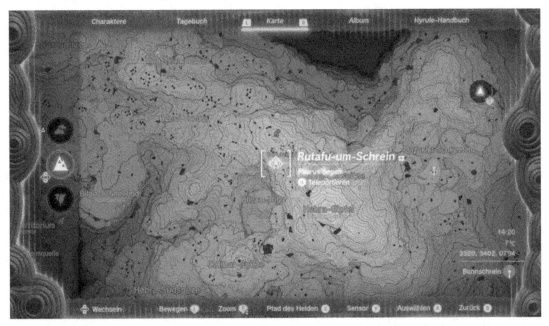

The entrance to the cave is almost directly next to Selmie's hut, northwest of Hebra East Spire. Sail down and look out for a small indentation quite far up, that's where the Mayoi sits, which you slay for the Mayoi Sign.

Slide further down - otherwise you will injure yourself when you jump. Below you will find an ice-cold lake and further back a camp with four Bokblins. Defeat them and continue into the cave where you will find half a shrine. The glow from the missing crystal points to the lake in the cave.

Run around the lake on the left, pick up the maxi truffle on the wall, and melt the ice block to reveal a crate. At the entrance of the cave you will find a long icicle that you take with you. Connect it to the crystal in the lake and take both to the shrine. It opens and you receive the chest and the blessing light without having to solve another task.

Ejut-ume Shrine

Location: Hebra, Hebra Mountains, Minfla's Secret Spring
Thread: Naked Survival - Sneaked

The shrine is south of the Hebra North Face and west of Minfla's Secret Spring, the body of water marked there. The easiest way to see and reach the shrine is from above, a rock face shields it from views from the south. In this shrine, your equipment will be taken from you for the duration of the trial. So stock up on weapons on the left before the passage. Defeat all constructs in the shrine. You can sneak up, but you don't have to. The constructs will sound an alarm once you're spotted, but they'll calm down if you're out of sight.

Among other things, you can take the spiked barriers on the floor to the entrance of the interior to drop them on enemies' heads and graze the rest of the room for arrows. However you do it - when all constructs are defeated, the door to the chest and blessing light will open.

Ta'ujosi-puni Shrine

Locality: Hebra, Hebra Mountains
Thread: Forward or backward?

The shrine is located northwest of the tower at Karuga Pass in the snowy mountains at the edge of the map. The easiest way to see and reach it from the air is to glide there. Use the tower or the sky islands. In the first room, turn back the ball at the top of the ramp with the time reversal so you can run up. Once there, you'll see a crate falling over and over onto a wheel and crashing into the abyss. Just grab it with the Ultra Hand at the right moment and get a bow for it.

Now you stand on the switch on the ground so that the lock prevents the ball from falling into the hole. Then put the second ball next to you behind the stopped ball. Don't leave the switch! Once that's done, you use the time reversal on the front ball so that the back one is pushed into the switch.

In the next room, our solution might be a bit unorthodox - but it works. Take the ball from the room before and squash it into the left sloping rail to stop the falling switch ball. Then glue both of them together so that they don't roll any further. Now you can take both balls in one go, separate them below and put the switch ball in the switch.

For the last puzzle, put the ball in the moving basket on the right when it's close enough. Let him slide over the switch and then rewind the time of the ball - not the basket! Hovering the ball over the switch will stop the time reversal and it will fall into the appropriate hole. The path to the light of blessing is now free.

Location: Hebra, Hebra Mountains, Base of Torpor
Topic: Naked Survival - Feint

The cave is in the north-west of the map at the foot of the torpor, you have to slide or climb down. Watch out for the bears here, then look out for a cave entrance blocked by ice. Use a campfire or fire arrows to open the entrance. Inside you can light the campfire on the ground, but then the two frozen Bokblins will thaw.

Be sure to melt the ice blocking the further path into the cave. In the next room, destroy the ice on the ground by jumping on it. You end up in a cave with three Bokblins. Defeat them and collect their equipment if necessary - they are well equipped. Then look around for a block of ice on the wall. Melt it and behind it you will find the Ottaka Shrine.

It is a shrine where you lose your equipment for the duration of your stay. Equip yourself with the weapons on the left before the passage.

Defeat all six constructs in the next room. Easier to do is ignite the dry leaves on the ground to explode the explosive barrels, destroy the brittle pillar when the enemies are underneath and more - here are some traps you can use to disable the constructs . Once you've done that, you'll get your equipment back and the door to the chest and blessing light will be open.

But now out of the cold and into warmer climes: Off to Eldin and Akkala! In contrast to Hebra, you should pack the most airy clothes for the areas around Death Mountain, because it gets hot.

We also provide you with our shrine walkthrough in this large area, but due to the sheer size of the game, it will unfortunately take a while before the guide is 100% complete. We thank you for your patience! And now on to Eldin and Akkala, check shrines!

All Shrines - Eldin & Akkala

Tired of cold, snow and poor visibility? Then you might enjoy the shrine tour of our walkthrough in Eldin and Akkala. We're gradually adding shrines if you're currently missing a copy - we're working flat out to complete the guide! But let's move on, pack your things and head to Eldin and Akkala in northeast Hyrule. You can use the table of contents to jump to individual shrines or work through them one by one.

Location: Eldin, Eldin Gorge
Theme: Against the current

The shrine is located north of Goronbi Lake on the hillside, it is easily accessible from the air. In the first room, simply jump from lava slab to lava slab to get to the other side. Now you see a switch for a ball in front of you in the ground. To get to it, you fish two long and one short lava plate and glue them together lengthwise. You now wedge it diagonally into the lava channel to block the flow. More plates accumulate, so you can run to the ball and further back to the right to the box. Then take the ball to the switch. Now grab a lava plate and take it through the door.

For this you have to squeeze a bit and twist them. Strap on two fans and let yourself be driven comfortably to the blessing light. There are two hydrants at the top of the platform, but you don't need them to solve the puzzle.

Location: Eldin, Eldin Gorge
Topic: wind force

First take a fan, turn it flat and let it fall down from as far up as you can at the platform with the crate on the left. Then stand on it and turn back time to get the contents of the chest.

Now strap the fans to the rotating mechanism on the outside on opposite sides and turn them on so that it spins in circles and activates the air switches. The light of blessing is already yours!

Domsu'ino Shrine

Location: Akkala, Akkala Plateau
Topic: Hidden path

The shrine sits high on the ruins of the Akkala Fortress. You can easily see and reach it from the tower. Use the ceiling jump when the path ends. Hit the switch and run into the metal box once the door is on your side. In this room you press the switch again. Stop and press it again.

Now you get through an opening to a box. Go back to the switch and hit it again.

Now there is another box right next to the switch - but you can also reach it directly with the ceiling jump when you enter the room for the first time.

To get the third crate, look out for another platform with a crate. Stand next to it as soon as the platform and crate are at ground level and press the switch from there with an arrow.

Now turn until the opening on the side is in such a way that you can activate the first switch outside the room with an arrow. Do that and then look inside the room for the long pillar. You have to perform the ceiling jump on her to get to the end of the shrine. Just keep turning until you can jump through them and get a blessing light when you get to the top.

Maya Tjidegin Shrine

Location: Eldin, Eldin Gorge
Theme: Naked Survival - Hunted

The shrine is on a rise northwest of the Akkala South Stable. It is again a battle shrine. You get your equipment back when you leave the shrine or once you have defeated all enemies. How you do that is up to you. You are simply not allowed to die - but beware, your food has also been confiscated for the duration of the trial.

Use the weapons on the left in front of the entrance and activate the small tanks with one blow. You can strap all sorts of items to the tanks that you find in the large room afterwards or that the opponents lose. Let your creativity run free - the shrine is really fun. At the end, as usual with shrines of this type, you will receive a chest and a blessing light.

Sin-natakk Shrine

Location: Akkala, Akkala Plateau
Theme: Combat Techniques: Raid

You can find this shrine northwest of the great chasm in the plains of East Akkala. You can see it well from the Marcuse Peninsula, but from the other direction it is shielded by rocks. In this scream you have to attack the construct with raid attacks. To do this, sneak behind enemies and press the Y button.

Once you have to surprise a stationary construct, once a patrolling one. You get access to the box automatically with the blessing light. Pull out all the stops in this test if you have to - take stealth medicine, wear your stealth clothes, there is no special strategy - then the blessing light will be yours.

Gemimiq Shrine

Location: Akkala, Sea of Akkala, Marcuse Peninsula
Theme: firepower

The shrine is located on the distinctive, donut-shaped Marcuse Peninsula in East Akkala. You can see it from the air and you can walk to it or hover from the tower. Glue the propeller to the round device and place a plate to bypass the current. With the updraft of the fan you now glide up and take a flamethrower. Glue it to the fan so that its rotation will ignite all the torches.

The path to the Light of Blessing is now clear, but you still want to get the crate that is further up, opposite the platform with the flamethrowers. Let yourself be carried as far up as possible with the fan.

It will probably take a few tries to get the momentum and direction right. If you know a better solution, let us know in the comments - but after a couple of failed launches, we were able to pick the box using this method.

Joti-i'u Shrine

Location: Akkala, Inner Akkala
Topic: Zugzuzug

The shrine is clearly visible just next to the East Akkala stable on the way to the institute. To your left in the first room is a platform with a crate, in front of you is a Jenga tower and there is a switch that doesn't get power. Below, closer to the tower, you can also see why: the connection is broken. So take two pieces of metal out of the tower without causing it to collapse and bridge the power grid.

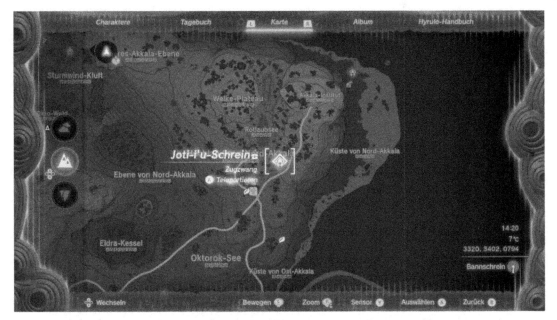

There is also a crate in the Jenga tower. If you pulled out the piece she was standing on she should now be at the bottom of the tower and you can grab her from the bottom with the Ultra hand. Or you can take them as soon as the power switch has activated the moving platform. Drive over and then get the orb to put it in the switch and open the door to the blessing light.

Now you grab the two Jenga parts that previously bridged the circuit and build a staircase slightly offset from them to open the second box on the platform on the wall. Now you can pick up the blessing light and the shrine is checked.

Kamtu-kisa Shrine

Location: Akkala, Inner Akkala
Theme: Perfect Shot

The shrine is located in Inner Akkala on the east bank of Skull Pond. It's easy to get to from the sky. When you get to the shrine, put the block on the mallet and pull the self-made hammer up and back. Release to play the ball into the round switch at the desired angle. You can use the column switch to let out a new ball if you miss. Once you hit, the door to the blessing light will open.

To open the chest in this shrine, you still have to go left. Basically the same task is waiting there again, but the goal moves back and forth. You can also try this task as many times as you want. With the switch you get a new ball. If you have mastered the test, the lattice behind which the treasure chest is open and you have completed the shrine.

Location: Akkala, Sea of Akkala
Theme: boost

You'll find the shrine on the beach north of the Akkala Institute on the northeast tip of Hyrule. Because it is shielded by the high rocky cliffs, it is difficult to see from the air and from the south and west.

Place the orb under the large slab in the first room. Cut the rope so she falls onto the ball. You can now push both together under water. The ball floats and makes the platform bounce upwards. Rewind time and jump onto the slab when it's underwater so that as soon as it comes up you'll get to the other side.

After that you lift the ramp up, let it fall again, rewind it and then run up to the other side. Run around the corner and build a raft out of two balls and the plate. Put the fan on and drive a little.

Shoot the crate dangling from the halfway wall and salvage it from the water. Then continue to the other shore, pick up an orb and place it on the switch. Your path to the Light of Blessing is now free.

Igasuk Shrine / Coastal Cave of North Akkala

Location: Akkala, Sea of Akkala, Ireland
Theme: Raurus blessing

This shrine stands in the middle of the so-called Irrland in North Akkala off the coast - the striking building looks like a maze. The fastest way to get to the shrine is through the coastal cave in North Akkala. The entrance is opposite the Mainland Fortress near the Rasi-waka Shrine.

Fight your way through the cave and at the end jump through the pillar where the Mayoi is sitting and into the huge room.

If you don't feel like a hard fight, just jump through another of the many broken columns onto the roof here.

Orientate yourself on the map: you want to go behind the large, dark box in the middle of the building.

Run to the edge and drop down the north side of the massive part of the structure. Enter below and turn to reveal a treasure chest.

In this treasure chest you use the ceiling jump and run up the stairs until you come to the shrine. Kindly enough, there are chests and blessing lights "free" - you don't have to solve any other tasks or puzzles.

Location: Akkala, Taburasa
Theme: Raurus blessing

The shrine stands by the waterfall in the south of Lake Akkala. However, the shrine is not complete, the crystal is missing. You can find it in Taburasa, it's for sale.

Bargain with the seller to save money. Then take the crystal and take the railroad down to the project site.

There's a lot of stuff there to build a raft. Ship the crystal over to the shrine and you'll receive a chest and a blessing light without having to complete another task.

Rashtaki-waka Shrine

Location: Akkala, Akkala Plateau
Theme: Bare Survival - Motorized

The shrine is located south of Taburasa on the Akkala Plateau and can be seen clearly from the settlement. Just run over to reach him, of course you can also do it from the air.

As always with these battle shrines, you lose your clothing, weapons, and shields for the duration of the trial.

You have to take care of yourself and thus defeat all construct opponents in the shrine without healing yourself - you don't have any food in your pocket either. How exactly you proceed is up to you, the main thing is that you survive. You don't have to go looking for a crate either, it's in the room with the blessing light once you've mastered the task

Shortly after the entrance on the left you can equip yourself with the most necessary things, then you are on your own. Running over the enemies here is the funniest thing - there's a fully equipped vehicle in the back left.

We are working diligently to complete the walkthrough for all shrines. In the meantime, you can continue with our guide to the shrines in Necluda! On the next page we have gathered all the shrines that we have discovered and solved there (so far).

Roll up your sleeves, there is also a lot for you to do in Necluda and lots of blessings to bag.

All Shrines - Necluda & Ranelle

Beautiful Necluda and Ranelle include Kakariko and Hateno, larger settlements worth visiting - but we're here for the shrines first. Looking for the shrines in the Sky Isles? Of course we also have them ready for you - at least in part, due to the size of the game our complete solution is inevitably a work in progress - further down we dedicate a separate page in our walkthrough to the shrines in the sky.

Tsuqarok Shrine

Location: Ranelle, Ranelle Swamp
Theme: push forward

The shrine is in the grove south of Rebona Bridge on the east side of the Hylia River. First you come into a large room. Run through to the end and then go down where there is a large ball.

Glue them to the vehicle, place it in the middle of the lava and let yourself be driven over.

When you get there, take the ball and stick it on the block on the right, which is sitting on a rail. Grab the stone slab leaning against the wall and place it on the sloping pipes in the upper area. Use the ceiling jump to jump onto the slab, grab the sliding platform with your ultra hand and slide it all the way to the other side.

Hold them there for a moment and exit the plate. The rail with the ball moves back, but that's okay.

Now hop up with the ceiling jump where the rail ends and use the time reversal to let the ball go up again. Then just grab them with the Ultra Hand and you've mastered this room too.

Take the orb to the next room where you will find rafts and water. Go to the separated channel between the two rafts and first fish the chest out of the water. Then you take a raft and put the ball as exactly in the middle as possible.

Now you place the raft on the tires on the narrow rails of the channel and activate the wheels with an arrow.

The formation will be a little clumsy, but will still arrive safely on the other side. You take the ladder yourself. Press the switch on the other bank, take the ball through the gate and place it in the hollow so that you can reach the blessing light.

Jonzahu Shrine

Location: Ranelle, Ranelle Swamp
Theme: depth

The shrine is on Melka, the largest island in the Ranelle Swamp. In the first room put the big ball under the target in the water, it will jump up and open the gate.

In the next room you first get the box out of the water, which can be found there on the bottom left. Then take the bullet with you and don't be caught off guard by the construct opponent coming around the corner. Now do the same thing again and take the plate into the next room.

The riddle is very easy to solve there: Place the plate under the structure in the water, climb on it and climb up with the jump in the ceiling. Run to the exit and the blessing light is yours.

Zuzbi'e Shrine / Fountain of Adeya

Location: Necluda, Western Necluda
Theme: Raurus blessing

The fountain is located on the teardrop-shaped large island in Lake Adeya. Climbing without proper medicine is difficult here due to the constant dripping of water from the ceiling. You see a shrine glowing, but on the way there you encounter an Iwarok whose weak point can be found on its back. Work him until he's defeated. There is more to get in the cave. Look for a glowstone high up in the ceiling. Blast away the brittle rocks next to it with a bomb arrow and climb up - preferably drink anti-slip medicine - and get the maxi truffle and the crate there. In addition, a wooden board floats in the water at the robbed slime. Take it and face the wall from the robbed slime rock. Activate the Ultra Hand, then a crate will be highlighted in color. Place the raft and recover the crate from there, a bow awaits you. Then you look for a light mushroom on the wall. Next to it is a small indentation in the rock face. Grab the Maxi Truffle and the Thunder Flower.

Graze all other thunder flowers and ore chunks, if you want, then climb the - fortunately - short way up to the Zuzbi'e shrine. You don't have to fight or puzzle there, Raurus blessing will give you a box with a magic wand and a blessing light.

Makasura Shrine

Location: Necluda, Western Necluda, Kakariko
Theme: Up and down, back and forth

The puzzle items in this shrine are roly-poly figures. First jump up with the ceiling jump. There you will find an L-shaped lattice and two pop-up figures. When activated, they always stand up straight and no longer fall over. As usual, you activate and deactivate the constructs by hitting them.

Take the assembled part, activate the manikin and place it on the edge of the ravine. Climb up the grate and slide over. There you take the other lattice with the roly-poly and place it on the left of the lattice bars to climb up and get to the other side. Connect the roly-poly to the lattice lying here. Then rotate it so that you are catapulted to the chest at the top end of the room to get Fairy Water. Now turn the construct over, place the ball in the bowl and activate the man so that it flies over the partition and rolls into the switch. Now go to the other side and get the grate.

You strap that to the top of the roly-poly with bars that's still here. Now catapult yourselves to the other side: stand in the hemisphere and activate the roly-poly so that it stands up and you fly to the blessing light.

Moga-waka Shrine

Location: Ranelle, Village of the Zora
Theme: hydropower

The shrine stands in the middle of the village of Zora, which can be easily seen on the map as the prominent, ring-shaped, huge structure in the lake. Enter the shrine and turn right. There is a crate in the water, take it out with the ultra hand and open it.

Stay here and put the piece floating in the water on the wheel opposite the other and move it once with the ultra hand to the stream of water so that it starts spinning and produces electricity. Take the battery lying around in the room and charge it at your mini hydroelectric power station by placing it on the circle marked in yellow.

Take her to the opposite side. You can see another box behind a lattice. Put the battery down briefly on the ground and move the iron balls close together in the water. They don't have to touch. Then place the battery on the mark here and the current will flow. This opens the lattice door and you get to the crate. Make sure you swim around the outside of the load, then nothing can happen to you.

Now take your battery to the middle. Stand in the elevator and place the battery in the holder from there so that you can be brought up comfortably and receive the blessing light there.

Ihen-a Shrine

Location: Ranelle, Mipha's Source
Theme: In Limbo

You can see the shrine on top of the mountain very well from the Sky Islands Archipelago of Ranelle - shoot up the tower in Zorana Highlands and glide the track. The entrance of the temple is polluted with mud. Shower him with a well-aimed water fruit toss and enter him.

In the first room you simply build a staircase out of the floating platforms and keep going. Take the hover platform and place it nicely in the middle of the gap in the floor. Don't forget to activate it by hitting it or it will just fall down. Then put the grid on the platform and walk over. Take the platform with you and tilt it to get to the next floor. Here you can see a ball on a pedestal, a switch and other floating platforms. Take a platform and place it on the ledge at the top left next to the entrance to the room in order to reach the treasure chest there by jumping onto the platform.

Then you take the orb, stick it on a hover platform and send it over by flipping the switch. You then do the same with yourself: stand on a platform in front of the thruster, activate the switch with an arrow and hover over. Put the ball in the socket and you will receive your well-deserved blessing.

O-ogin Shrine / South Ranelle Road Cave

Location: Ranelle, Source of Ranelle
Theme: Raurus blessing

Below the Ranelle Plateau, set into the steep gorge, stands the O-ogin Shrine, which is missing the crystal. The light points to the waterfall opposite. Swim to the right side of the lake where the pillar fragments are and enter the South Ranelle Road cave. Climb further along the edge, the ground has broken away.

Behind the blue rocks is a glider and a gem, behind the brown rocks is the crystal. But watch out, behind the waterfall on the left, an electro-robbery slime wants to get at you. Go through the water, kill him, and follow the path to the end to collect the Mayoi Sign.

Then go back and through the right waterfall to open a chest. Now you get the crystal, build a glider with the material on site and fly relaxed over to the shrine, where you can get the blessing light and chest without having to solve any more puzzles.

Djogo-u Shrine / East Ranelle Road Cave

Location: Necluda, Eastern Necluda
Theme: Raurus blessing

The shrine is underground north of the Lake of Purification near the Naydra Snowfield. However, the entrance to the cave is on the slope of the Ranelle Mountains north of the shrine at the bottom of the cliffs. It goes steeply downhill, if you see a lonely column with Sonau balloon parts and further down one of the typical blue Rumi rabbits, you are correct.

The walls in the cave are slippery, so use the ceiling jump where you can. At the next slope, a stone robber slime is waiting at the top, dodge it or kill it. In the huge room that follows, the shrine lies within a lake in a hollow rock - difficult to reach because of the wet walls.

Walk around the shrine almost once and you'll see brittle rocks at the back. Use a Thunder Flower Arrow to blast your way to the shrine and just swim across. In the shrine you don't have to do any more tasks, you just get chest and blessing light.

Saquzuk Shrine

Location: Ranelle, Ranelle Point / Archipelago of South Ranelle
Topic: Naked Survival - Lifted off

You make this shrine visible by visiting a sky island and completing a snowboard route within a time limit. Blast your way into the sky with the tower on Ranelle Peak. Then fly to the sky island with the crescent shaped body of water on it. Interact with the seal and a target will appear at the end of the ramp.

Grab the sled shield at the edge (or use your own shield) and sled down. To use this move you have to press ZL, X and then A. The light falls to the ground, sliding a bit so you don't die on impact. Then follow the objective until the Saquzuk Shrine appears.

As with all Survival-themed Shrines, you will lose your equipment for the duration of the Trial. Help yourself to the left at the entrance with the weapons provided. Your goal is to defeat all constructs. Ride the balloons up, rewind the gondolas, or use the ceiling jump - all you have to do is climb up while eliminating all enemies.

Take their guns away, screw the stuff around to your reasoning amps (like the missiles in the room with the laser), and you'll be victorious. You don't have to look for the chest, it's in the room with the blessing light that opens when all constructs are history.

Eshoze Shrine

Location: Necluda, Western Necluda
Theme: Combat Techniques: Shield

The shrine is on the east side of the north twin mountain on the hillside. It is easy to see from the air (at least if you look in the direction from the east) and to reach it, and the path is also not a problem on foot if you walk around the twin mountain in the north. The stable of the Twin Mountains is right next to it.

The shrine is a battle shrine, you're probably already familiar with it: follow the instructions to defeat the construct enemy. If you are successful, you will gain access to the Light of Blessing and the chest.

Parry the throw with ZL and then A to claim the win. The timing can be a bit tricky, practice makes perfect. And don't fret if you use up a shield for this task: there's a good new shield waiting in the crate.

Tokjo'u shrine / cave at Eichsee

Location: Necluda, Western Necluda
Theme: Raurus blessing

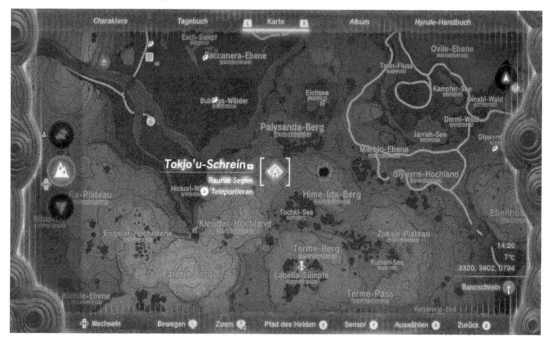

The entrance to the cave is north of the large abyss there on the east side of the Eichsee.

In the corridor you will first find an electronic robbery slime. You will then come to a room with an abandoned crystal. Collect the resources and then activate it. A gate opens and gives a clear view of your path - but peppered with lots of rolling boulders.

Better carry the crystal with the Ultra hand than the traditional way, then you can run faster, have a better view and it's easier to dodge. Put the crystal down at the end of the gauntlet and look for light sources on the slope of the path you just walked, there is a treasure chest there.

Go deeper into the cave. After the narrow passage, turn left and swim through the crevice (leave the crystal on the way). This is where the Mayoi lives that you slay for the Mayoi Sign. Return to the crystal and go down the other path. A boulder will roll towards you, rewind it and turn in the crystal at Tokjo'u Shrine to receive a chest and a blessing light as thanks. Before you leave the cave through the jump in the ceiling, you should still pocket the maxi precious truffle and the ore.

Sanmikka Shrine

Location: Necluda, East Necluda, Hateno
Theme: creation

The shrine is in the middle of Hateno, the city in eastern Hyrule. You can reach it on foot or from the air, the whole city is perfectly visible from the sky. Enter the shrine, there is a large room in front of you. Go down and use the Ultra Hand to dig through the sea of balls.

That's where the chest is. Now you build a shovel on the big wheel, with which one or more balls can be picked up. Either you put a plate in the middle and surround it with side plates so that the ball doesn't roll out, or you build a wider shovel out of four plates.

Then you might have to try the whole thing twice if the balls roll unfavorably, but in principle the shape of your shovel doesn't matter.

You only have to pick up the fifth plate, because you put it on the yellow glowing cable to connect it to the wheel and activate it. Now go up the ladder and look forward to a ball rolling into the switch. The door will open and the blessing light will be yours.

Mayan hishka shrine / cave in Expa Forest

Location: Necluda, East Necluda, Hateno
Theme: Raurus blessing

Follow the path from Hateno to the institute and before the last bend look at the small group of trees directly below the institute. You see brittle rocks that you have to destroy to get into the cave. An unobstructed entrance is at the bottom of Sumac Lake in the forest.

If you run all the way down, you will find the Mayoi on the ceiling, which you kill for the Signum. Then you turn back and enter the Mayan hishka shrine. You don't have to solve a puzzle in it; The box and blessing light are yours when you enter the shrine.

Djodj'u-u Shrine

Location: Necluda, Western Necluda, Ubota Plateau
Topic: bridge building

The shrine is on a plateau right next to the stable by the lake. First you go over the bridge. Then you glue the next bridge to the intended bridge post. It's getting a little more complicated now: The bridge is too long and sags, so you can't reach the further path. So do not take the last link of the suspension bridge to glue it, but an earlier one. Now you need to weigh down the bridge so it's taut enough to use. To do this, roll it out and glue the stone block that is standing around. Place the bridge over the staff and the block will tighten it, allowing you to progress. Now comes the last bridge: Run in the direction of the exit, but turn around in front of it and glue the middle of the bridge to the platform above to get to the chest. Now you get the blessing you deserve.

Sif Mim Shrine

Location: Necluda, Eastern Necluda
Theme: Naked Survival - In the Flow

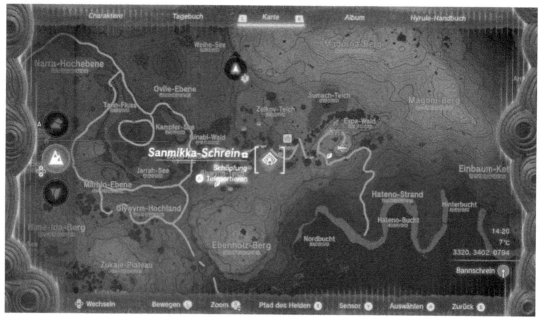

The shrine is just before Angelstedt, east of the stable of the lake. You can see it well from the tower at Labella Swamp. It is also easy to reach on foot by following the road east from Stall am See. There are two NPCs camping next to the shrine who have a quest for you - but it has nothing to do with the shrine. As usual in Battleshrines, you will lose all your gear for the duration of the trial and will have to equip yourself with whatever you find along the way. The goal is to overwhelm all enemies. How you turn off the constructs is entirely up to you.

Inconveniently, there is no bow in the weapon rack just before the entrance to the chamber. You have to grab it from a construct first. The rafts in the water that enemies look out for are destructible.

And since constructs can't swim, you should take advantage of that - push them into the water and you'll set the raft on fire. You don't have to look for a box here, it's at the exit by the blessing light when you've defeated all enemies.

Bamitok Shrine / Cave at Daskida Mountain

Location: Necluda, Eastern Necluda
Theme: Raurus blessing

The cave entrance is the body of water east of Angelstedt (not the small pond in the village, but the larger one on the map). You have to swim a bit into the entrance area. Inside, a Horrorblin and a chest await you behind Roots. In the next room there are two electro-robber slimes lurking.

Defeat them, but before taking the path deeper into the cave, look around for a narrow passageway half-hidden by roots. Behind it is the Mayoi, which gives you another Mayoi sign if you kill him. Then go further down into the cave. Don't forget to pick up the ore and maxi truffle along the way. The next room has many vertical levels. If you want to climb up, you need a lot of stamina or special equipment such as anti-slip medicine or appropriate clothes, because the cave is dripping from the ceiling and everything is slippery and wet. At the top is a chest with a King's Shield and the shrine you're probably headed for.

So try to get up the moss wall somehow, look for ceiling jump opportunities, defend yourself against the two rock robbery slimes on the slope and enter the Bamitok shrine. Because the path was so difficult and the shrine is so hidden, you don't have to take another exam. You get a chest and the blessing light just like that. Now you can explore the rest of the cave below if you wish.

Mayan ri'ina shrine / Cave of Jotwerde

Location: Necluda, Sea of Necluda, Jotwerde
Theme: Raurus blessing

The island of Jotwerde is located southeast of Hyrule. An NPC there gives you the task of eliminating the island's monster camps. As part of this mission you will also run into the shrine. So the pirates are said to have a secret hiding place on the back of the island...

Whether you complete the NPC mission or not: The plateau is hollow on the sea side and includes an entire pirate ship. You can hardly see it from above or from the sides. But you can see it very clearly if you look at Jotwerde from the small reef to the east - then you can also take the Krog with you, which runs in circles there. Swim into the cave and eliminate the monsters.

The shrine stands in a bay behind the ship and the entrance is protected with spikes. Don't even try to float in and instead lay the planks down so you can walk across. You no longer have to complete a task in the shrine, the chest and the blessing light are yours as soon as you enter the shrine.

Those were - for now! - all shrines in our Zelda: Tears of the Kingdom walkthrough in Necluda and Ranelle. But as you know, Hyrule encompasses many more areas. So we continue to work our way south, to Phirone. Here, too, lights of blessing await brave heroes who solve the tasks in the shrines. So turn the page and follow us south.

All Shrines - Phirone & Gerudo

Not too cold, not too warm - Phirone is bearable. It's a little bit sunny in south-western Gerudo. Of course, in Zelda: Tears of the Kingdom, there are also some shrines with tasks waiting for brave adventurers. So that you can find and master the shrines without any problems, our walkthrough walkthrough continues. Jump to shrines that interest you, or just go through the list from top to bottom. And if there's a shrine missing that you're stuck in - we're constantly updating the guide. And off we go into the kingdoms of Phirone and Gerudo.

Jiukum Shrine

Location: Phirone, Phirone Prairies
Subject: Exact fit

The shrine is north of Lake Dracoto on a rise. It is easy to see and reach from the air, more specifically from the tower in Cottonwood Highlands. In the first room, glue the two panels together, place them on the rails and slide down the panel.

In the next room, look to the left where the three square tiles are. A crate is on a platform separated from you by rails. Put one slab in the back and a second slab in front. Glue the third panel to the back one, slightly inclined so that you can walk up it. Now take one of the small slabs and hang it between the rails at the bottom of the wider slab that falls onto the rails at the top. Stand on it and let yourself be driven over. Now you take the rectangular plate and put the three square plates on the bottom, one on the outside and one in the middle.

Place the M-shaped piece on the rails and place a fan on the platform you are standing on above each of the small plates. Activate the fans and let them drive you over to the blessing light.

En Omha Shrine / Whirlpool Cave in Lake Hylia / Shrine in Lake Hylia / Archipelago of Phirone

Location: Phirone, Lake Hylia
Theme: Raurus blessing

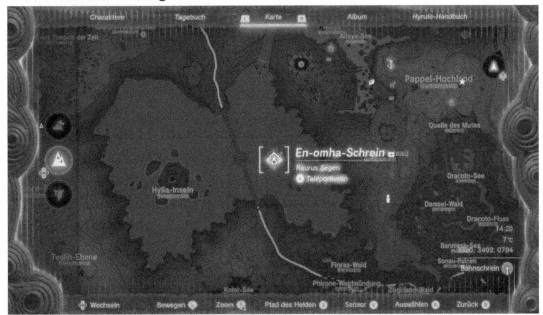

The crystal of the shrine can be found on a sky island on the right in the Phirone archipelago. You can get there by flying over from the tower in Poplar Highlands, preferably with the help of Tulin. The missing crystal is inside the building in the middle of the island. Activate it and throw it into the hole in front of you.

Jump down and let the whirlpool take you to the whirlpool cave in Lake Hylia. Bring the crystal the few more steps to the shrine and you will receive the chest and the blessing light without having to solve any more puzzles. Still take care of the Mayoi sign when you step out of the shrine.

Usshok Shrine

Location: Phirone, Phirone Prairies
Theme: Vertical and horizontal

The shrine is in close proximity to the Mesa Stables. In the first room, lift the "paddle" behind the ball up and let go so it pushes the ball over the rails and into the switch. In the next room, put the block on the paddle, but not quite flush with the bottom or it won't pull back far enough. Then you do the same as in the room before - shoot the ball into the switch.

If you want to open the chest in the third room, it gets a bit more complicated. Take the plate and put it on the paddle, pushing the ball back onto the switch. Now a cart falls on the other rails. Now put the plate on the other side of the paddle and send the empty cart to the other side.

As she slowly drives back, you release the plate from the paddle. As soon as the cart is back, put the plate flat on top, stand on it and turn back time - make sure you get the cart and not the plate. Now you can hop from the slab to the chest. You can get to the light of blessing simply by standing in the cart and lifting the paddle from the cart.

Ishokin Shrine

Location: Phirone, Phirone Prairies
Theme: Raurus blessing

The shrine missing the crystal is west of Nesuppo Forest in Phirone on the mountain. The crystal isn't far away, you can find it on the neighboring mountain top where a fire is burning. Unfortunately, the NPC camping there doesn't give you the crystal just like that. He wants to see a giant horse. You will receive a side quest and should now stop by the plateau stables.

Teleport to the shrine next to it or travel east along the road. Phanna tells you about a giant white horse at the Lake of the Horse God here, so that's your next target.

Cross the bridge at the Horse God's Lake and you'll see the two men camping out looking for the giant white horse. If you continue to follow the path, you will see the giant mold surrounded by butterflies. Tame him - but you need a lot of stamina for this, so you may have to level up first and come back later. In any case, the reward for your efforts is a chest and a blessing light.

Motusij Shrine

Location: Gerudo, Gerudo Plateau, Southern Irregular Castle
Theme: Raurus blessing

The shrine is located in the southern madhouse in Gerudo. You can get to him by following the acorns and bird nuts scattered by a researcher. Or you can just jump down at the spot we marked on the map. In the shrine you will receive the chest and the light of blessing without having to take another test.

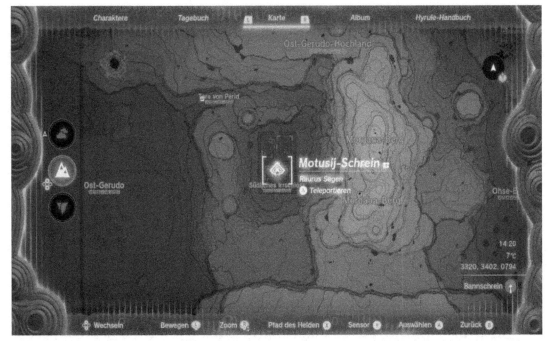

After that, interact with the relic and the southern lunatic castle in the sky will be accessible. Another shrine awaits you there, you can read more about it in our walkthrough for shrines on the Sky Islands on the following page of our walkthrough.

Kita-waka Shrine

Location: Gerudo, high plateau of Gerudo
Theme: Creative Wayfinding

The shrine is located in Gerudo, high on a mountain and to the east of the great chasm on the map.

It can be seen from afar and is very easy to reach from the air. First stick the plate that is on the right side of the wall in front of half the bridge that is pointing up and run over it. Take the piece off again and glue it to the gear on the left so you can get to the crate.

Take the piece back with you and stick it to the half bridge on the right so you can walk on it. Now you take the other plate there on the ground and stick it on at an angle so that you can walk up to the next platform.

You can shorten the third puzzle simply by taking the ramp you just attached below, holding it up horizontally with the ultra hand, dropping it, stepping on it, rewinding time and allowing it to bring you up. The light of blessing is yours!

Now we come to the last chapter of our shrine solution in Zelda: Tears of the Kingdom. For this we rise high in the air to visit the shrines above Hyrule. The cartography towers are always good starting points for the tour above the clouds. Or you can use balloons and time reversal on falling rocks to climb to the top. See you on the next page!

All Shrines - Sky Islands

Yes, you can also find Shrines (and Krogs) across Hyrule. Why this walkthrough for TloZ: TotK doesn't include the abyss? There are no shrines there - but where there are shrines on the upper world, you will find the roots under the earth where you reveal the card.

It is therefore very useful to uncover as many shrines as possible. But anyway, now it's off to the top.

Here comes our solution for all shrines in the Sky Isles of Tears of the Kingdom. One more note: the four shrines on the Forgotten Skyislands, the starting area of Tears of the Kingdom, can be found at the beginning of the article (and in our separate walkthrough for this part of the game), because you have to complete them anyway to get the to enter the open world. All the shrines here can only be reached afterwards.

Djindoka'o Shrine

Location: Archipelago of South Hyrule
Theme: Raurus blessing

The shrine is missing its crystal. You can get there via the Forgotten Sky Isles, the starting area. Teleport there to the western shrine and float over, preferably with Tulin's help.

There you can advance with the materials on site, such as gliders and the hover blocks with rockets. Follow the beam of light and use the Ultra Hand to rotate the strange construct in front of you on its own axis so that the paths are connected. You can also see a treasure chest dangling from a rope, we'll take care of it afterwards.

So build the path and go over to the crystal. Be sure to take the maxi turnips with you! Then carry the crystal to the shrine and you'll receive a "free" blessing light and a chest that doesn't require you to solve any further puzzles.

Now you get the old map out of the box: Turn the construct so that the strut with the treasure chest is pointing vertically upwards and another way to you. You take it now, climb up, cut the chest and open it.

Locality: Archipelago of West Hebra
Topic: Not just defense

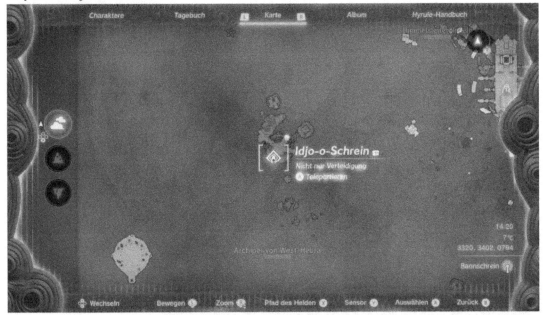

You can get to the sky from the tower at Karuga Pass. Land on one of the sky islands with a balloon stone nearby to go further up. From a certain height you can already see the shrine. Hover over and enter it. Defeat the Construct opponent and take the torch to melt the ice blocking the passage. Also defeat the next enemy and light your torch at the fire. Melt the ice to open the box. Now hold your shield in front of you - it doesn't have to be the enemy's, it just has to be fireproof - and go into the next room.

Defeat the third enemy as well, then use Synthesis to glue a missile to your shield. Then pull out the shield to be shot up. You can now easily glide to the Light of Blessing.

Tanino-ud Shrine

Locality: Archipelago of Eastern Hebra
Theme: Raurus blessing

The shrine is located on the Heavenly Islands in the Eastern Hebra archipelago. You can get there by being catapulted up from the tower in the Zuzukiki Snowfield. Glide to one of the islands and build a sky raft using the controller, batteries and fans. Watch out for the construct opponents who are waiting on other floating blocks and shooting at you with rockets. Keep going northeast until you get to the half shrine. You will also find a capsule machine with fans, sleds, transporters, headlights and gliders. Activate the shrine so the light points to the missing crystal. Allow the push mechanism to launch you onto the island.

If you want to recover the Ancient Map in the crate, drive up with one of the fan blocks, shoot it, then slide down onto the smaller island it landed on. Then come back up with the hot air balloons.

Slide down the edge of the island where a floating platform already stands. You see huge lianas, torch them. Also destroy the lianas behind it and you will find the crystal.

Now it gets pretty fiddly: Build fans and the control unit on the floating platform (don't forget the batteries too) and float up and then forward over the island towards the shrine Throw off the crystal when you are above solid ground. Then use the crystal and you will receive the chest and the blessing light without having to complete another trial.

Mayan um'kiza shrine

Location: Sky Ladder Islands
Topic: crucial point

You will inevitably pass by this shrine if you are following the story quest with Tulin in Hebra. He is in the Sky Ladder Isles in the storm.

Use the switch through the grate and enter the large room. Jump up on the ship and then jump to the next ship. Glide to the moving ship and jump again. Land on solid ground and look for a platform on the wall. There is a crate on top, you can get there by jumping onto a ship and gliding over.

Slide back and jump up with the ship so that you can use the switch behind the bars, whether with a weapon or a bow and arrow. Then use the ship directly below to reach the blessing light.

Kahatana-um Shrine

Location: Sky Ladder Islands
Theme: Raurus blessing

You will also inevitably come across this shrine if you follow the Tulin quest and ascend the Sky Ladder Islands in the storm. Convenient: It's a Raurus Blessing Shrine, so you don't have to fight or solve any puzzles and just get a chest and a Blessing Light.

Location: Archipelago of South Eldin
Theme: waterways

The shrine is on the South Eldin archipelago, with the tower nearby you can get there. Drive on the tracks and get the old map: When you reach the second island, look back, the crate is hanging down to the right of the tracks. Go further ahead and remove the lianas, use the ceiling jump, continue traveling by rail, then you have to slide and finally you end up at the shrine.

In the first room, take the lava plates on the right near the hydrant and build a path from them. Then take the lava floes and build a ramp to get to the crate on the left with a construct bow. Now you put a lava boulder with synthesis on a weapon or the sword that is next to the cracked wall and smash your obstacle.

Put a fire hydrant on the bridge in the next room and take the lava floes to build a long bridge out of them. Lay it across the canal so you can stand on it. Activate and grab the other fire hydrant so that you create platforms of cold lava as you move forward. The light of blessing is already yours.

Mogisari Shrine

Location: Irrland: Sky
Topic: high spirits to jump

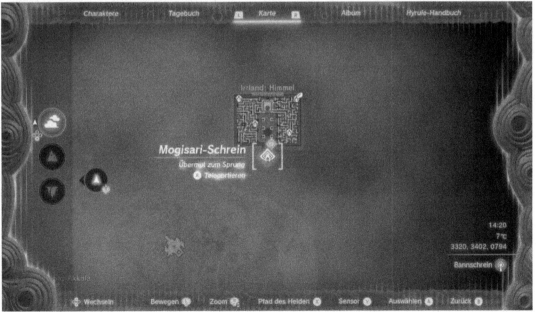

The shrine can be found in Northern Akkala's Sky-Ireland. First you have to reach the shrine in Earthly Irrland and interact with the gate in front of the huge structure, otherwise the switches inside will not work if you also want to complete the part of the quest in the abyss.

For example, using multiple balloons and high-capacity batteries, you can get high enough to enter the Irrland in the sky. The shrine stands at the gates of the huge maze. Because you're so high off the ground, there's less gravity here, and you can jump farther.

Take the right car in the shrine and speed towards the lava and ski jump. Jumps off at just the right moment to just about glide over. From here, jump and slide to the next level and over the spikes. Complete the two constructs. Stay on the top half and avoid the lasers by jumping and sailing over the finials on the edge. Also get rid of the next two construct archers and go to the broken wall. Behind it you will find the chest of the shrine. Also remove the last construct and build the four missiles on the car. Then you drive it over the gap to the blessing light.

Kumma'ino Shrine

Location: Archipelago of Necluda
Theme: Raurus blessing

The shrine is located on the Sky Isles in the Necluda Archipelago, slightly southeast of the tower in the Labella Marshes. This is how you get to the shrine: Let yourself be shot up and then float to the archipelago. There you use the floating platforms and trampolines. The shrine is missing the crystal, so interact with it to get the beam of light to guide you.

As luck would have it, the Gamma Construct Golem on the island next door has the crystal. Depending on your equipment and number of heart containers, the fight could be difficult, so prepare well.

When you're done, carry the crystal to the gap between the two islands and bring it and you safely across with a balloon and fan to unite it with the shrine. The blessing light and the contents of the chest are yours.

Raqasho-go Shrine

Location: Archipelago of East Gerudo
Topic: Reflected action

This shrine is located in the East Gerudo Archipelago and is easily accessible from the tower in Gerudo Valley. Atypical for shrines in the Sky Islands, you don't have to obtain a crystal, the shrine is complete. Go into the room downstairs and grab the mirror by the door. Hold it up so that the light is directed onto the target above the door. Hold the mirror until the hallway opens.

In the next room, take the mirror with the Ultra Hand, lift it through the opening in the lattice, and rotate it so the light hits the target again. Then leave the mirror in front of the door so that it reflects light through the gate and keep running.

Grab the mirror in the next room and turn it to activate the switch on the floor. Then you put this mirror in the beam of light and turn it up, but you don't put it on the moving platform, but in front of it. Drive up and grab the mirror by the block.

Stand on the moving platform with it and direct the light that shines upwards onto the target to make the room with the chest accessible.

Defeat the two constructs in the next room. Take one of the two mirrors here and position it so that it throws the light at an angle next to the pillars blocking the path. There you place the second mirror and turn it so that it hits the target. The path to the light of blessing is now free.

Djosiu Shrine

Location: Archipelago of North Necluda
Theme: Raurus blessing

This shrine is located on an archipelago of sky islands. We reached them by rewinding a falling boulder on a peak of Narisha Heights.

First look around up there, pick flowers and enjoy the view. Since the shrine is not complete, it does not glow. Look out for the typical "arms" around shrines. Once you have found it, you interact so that the light shows you where the missing crystal is.

The light points straight ahead. In front of you is a structure with which you can operate the curved bridge. Use the Ultra Hand so you can run and glide over to the crystal. Place the crystal on the ground in front of the bridge and return to the path controls.

Now turn the path so that it connects the island with the crystal to the left of it. To reach it, you have to turn the hydraulic mechanism on the island in front of the shrine, you can do that with physical strength. Let yourself be shot over, run to get the crystal and place it in the middle of the stone bridge.

Before you go back to the control box, you should take a look down from the bridge. You see a box dangling from a rope. Inside is another Old Map. Shoot the chest and get the contents before you run to the control mechanism one last time and now carefully turn the bridge so that you can run over and insert the crystal in the shrine.

Raurus' blessing means that you don't have to do anything in this shrine to get a box and a blessing light. One effort at the crystal was enough.

Jan'samino Shrine

Location: Necluda Airspace, Sonanium Plant Island
Thread: Naked Survival - Relieved

You can only reach this shrine if you have already obtained the Zora Armor in the Zora Village, which allows you to swim up waterfalls, and have a lot of stamina - or at least a lot of stamina-restoring food. If so, let the tower on Ranelle Spire launch you into the sky and then sail southwest.

On the map, the island you want to go to is lighter than the others and surrounded by rounded shapes. You have to fly into the waterfall so that you can swim up it - so put on the Zora armor beforehand. Once inside the waterfall, press the A Button to climb it. You arrive on a small island with a pond (with maxi carp and a treasure chest with an old map inside!) and fairies. Could be so nice, but a construct shoots missiles at you from a hover platform. Defeat it, clamp the two missiles lying around to the platform and drive over to the Sonanium Plant Island where the shrine is.

In order to achieve that, you have to pass another test. Activate the switch at the entrance to the island so the turbines blow air out of the pipes. Let yourself be carried up station by station until you have reached the middle. Look down the hole: Lasers everywhere!

You have to skilfully avoid the rays on the way when gliding down, but the wind from below pushes you up a little every time you cushion the fall with the sail. So be careful and carefully match the openings of the moving laser beams. At the bottom you are finally at the shrine, and a capsule machine with good content is also here.

One might think that with such an arduous journey you would just get a chest and a blessing light. It's not like that though, it's a battle shrine where, as usual, you'll lose all your equipment while your trial is taking place. After all, there's no hidden chest here, you'll get that after successfully completing your task.

As always, you can help yourself to the left of the entrance with makeshift equipment.

The theme of the shrine relates to gravity. Since you're so high up in the sky, you can jump further. Use all your tricks to defeat the construct opponents without dying. There are no specifications. Nice weapons can be synthesized with the parts lying around, so have fun. The constructs are distributed vertically in the room in case you don't find them all. At the end you collect your blessing light and the shrine is complete.

Jiru-tag'mats

Location: Ranelle Archipelago
Theme: Exhilarated

Blast your way up with the tower in Zorana Highlands. If you haven't activated the tower yet, help the Zora in front of it who's stuck in the slime by throwing a water fruit on the mud. Once you've been shot into the sky, you'll see a spinning orb below you.

Match the moment when the opening is facing up and slide inside. Stop the rotating mechanism by turning off the fan on it and enter the shrine.

Take the glider and use it to float left onto the next platform. Grab one of the small trolleys there and glue it to the bottom of your glider and fly across to the platform where there is a fan. You can also see a crate on a high platform from there. Take the glider and place it across the hole in the floor to jump to the crate from the glider.

Now all you have to do is attach the fan to your glider, bring it to the front of the ramp and glide over to the blessing light. Don't worry about the battery - you'll have unlimited juice in shrines, you'll definitely come across. Provided you don't fall off the glider.

WIND TEMPLE
WALKTHTROUGH

The Legend of Zelda: Tears of the Kingdom is finally out - and we really enjoyed the gameHere we give you a complete walkthrough for the temple that lies high above the clouds in freezing Hebra. The associated quest is called "Tulin of the Orni People" and you get it if you visit the Orni village in the northwest and talk to the NPCs there. You get to the Wind Temple by following Tulin's quest in Hebra and climbing the Sky Ladder Islands until you jump from above into the massive storm raging across the land. First of all: Destroy all the crates to bag as many arrows as possible and also take any fire fruit you find with you.

Wind Temple - five turbines

Once on the ship's deck, run north and then left. Flip the switch to open the door lock. Get the opal from the chest and jump up one floor. In the big icicle is another box with arrows. Go back downstairs and glue an icicle to the broken switch opposite the one you just flipped. Now you can kill him and enter the room next to it.

Stand in front of the turbine and let Tulin create a gust of wind to make it spin. Now run to the room on the other side of the ship. Stuck in the ice is a box containing a Beta Warrior Lance. Jump to the ceiling and destroy the turret by letting it target you. Once it fires, use Time Reverse to redirect the rock. Now do the same with the turret on the left outer side of the ship. With the elastic sails of the boats you come back up. Now you do the turret the same way on the right side as well. You'll find a bow in a box on a floating, semi-circular island. You can always use it, especially here with the approaching boss fight! From there you will see an opening full of icicles on the ship. jump and sail there

To your left is a crate behind a lattice. Shoot the large icicles on the ceiling, glue them together and use them to fish through the hole in the grate for the crate. Glue them to the ice, bringing them forward so you can lift and open them through the gap. A sapphire is now yours. On the other side, turn the reel around with the time reversal and allow yourself to be transported to the other side. Activate the switch.

Shoot down a long icicle and stick it between the gears on the wall as an extension to open the door. Behind you will find the next turbine. Jump back up through the ceiling onto the ship's deck. Now turn to the other side of the ship and enter the interior through the open entrance in the front top left. To your left you see laser beams and a construct opponent. Defeat the enemy and climb the walls so the lasers don't pick you up. In the box you will find a rhodonite.

Turn around. On the left are boxes with arrows and through the grid you can see a box that you will get later. Look on the opposite wall for an entrance with a ladder, you don't have to go far there either. Head towards the ice walls instead. Two Sonau capsules are stuck in the block of ice. Let a gust of wind carry you over from Tulin and flip the switch. Then defeat the Construct opponent ahead. Jump to the ceiling. In the next passage on the right in the indentation there is a box under the rubble in which you will find a weapon. Take the two fragments of the walls here with you further behind. Glue the parts to the hanging metal rod like wings on a pinwheel and tell Tulin to blow a gust of wind on it. The gate will open and you can go further up.

The fourth wind turbine is easy to activate: go back down the outside of the ship and stand on the wing of the ship closest to the center. Look towards the ship and you will see that there is another platform below. Let Tulin's gust carry you over, defeat the opponent, activate the turbine and then glide to the ladder.

Go back onto the ship's deck and now use Tulin and the ships to jump to the top of the ship. There you will see a locked gate. Open it with the Ultra Hand, below you'll see a Mission Impossible room with lasers. Jump down and use the glider to correct your course, but be careful, the wind will always push you back up. Land on the indentation and look around - you can see the crate from earlier in another indentation across the way. Glide over and you'll get a Sonau Broadsword. But now let's go to the last turbine, that was where you just landed. Activate them with Tulin and return to the center of the ship.

Boss fight: Frosgeira

Once you've activated all the turbines and return to the center of the ship, it's time for the boss fight. The monster Frosgeira's weak point is on its underside. Three circular areas glow purple there. You have to hit each of these spots with two fire arrows to damage Frosgeira. Otherwise, the fight is quite simple: fly around, occasionally dropping to be able to shoot at weak spots from below. Don't forget to photograph Frosgeira for your guide. To do this, you land on one of the pieces of debris floating on the edge of the storm. Once you have destroyed all three weak points, Frosgeira's second phase begins. He summons hurricanes that you dodge. If Frosgeira attacks from below, all you have to do is hover a bit out of the way then he presents his stomach including weak points. In phase two you have to destroy all three spots again and victory is yours.

FIND A NEW
WARRIOR'S ROBE

The Legend of Zelda: Tears of the Kingdom is the direct sequel to The Legend of Zelda: Breath of the Wild. Link's iconic outfit in Zelda: Breath of the Wild is well known; the blue warrior's robe can be seen in all promotional materials. And indeed, the outfit is also in Zelda: Tears of the Kingdom! Princess Zelda hid it well, but we'll tell you where the chic top was found.

New warrior's robe from Breath of the Wild

You can get a clue to the location of the new warrior's robe in Tears of the Kingdom if you visit Zelda's house in Hateno and look for her secret room in the well. There you can read in her diary where she hid the warrior's robe. Of course it's not the fine English way - that's why we'll just tell you directly where you can find the top. A visit to Zelda's hiding place is still worthwhile, because in the chest in the fountain you will find the hair tie that goes with the warrior's robe. You must head to Inner Hyrule, the area you land in after the Forsaken Skyislands. You need to get into the throne room of Hyrule Castle - unfortunately it's in the part of the building that's floating in the air. For example, you have to arrive by balloon, or you use the Zora ability, Swim up waterfalls if you already have the Zora armor. You can get this in Ranelle in Zora Village by talking to the village headwoman.

So if you've arrived in Hyrule Castle's U1, you walk in and you're already in the throne room. Next to the throne you see two large braziers with the remains of a campfire. Light them again with fire fruits, then a stone shifts at the altar and you get to the treasure chest below. The new warrior's robe is hidden there - does it look familiar to you? To enhance the outfit, you need exquisite materials - Princess Gentian and White Dragon Scales.

UNLOCK SAHASRA TOWER

As in Breath of the Wild, in The Legend of Zelda: Tears of the Kingdom you uncover map sections by activating the cartography towers and scanning the environment. However, you cannot simply enter and use all towers. Some of them require you to complete small quests. Most are self-explanatory and not particularly difficult, but the Sahasra Tower quest isn't quite as obvious as other areas in the game. We'll tell you what the Orni NPC Schnabuda actually wants to tell you!

Unlock the tower at Sahasra Hill

Arrived at the tower - it is east of the plain of Hyrule and on the way towards Kakariko - you see the Orni Schnabuda standing in front of the door of the tower. He notes that the door is stuck and tells you about a cave nearby where he used to like to pick mushrooms. The idea suggests that Link should gather mushrooms for him so that Schnabuda gains strength and pries open the door. But the game wants something else from you. First you go into the cave on Sahasra Hill, the entrance is southeast of the tower on the hillside. After uncovering the entrance, three Horroblins will be waiting for you.

Slay them and remove the other brittle stones. You come out on the other side of the cave. Decimate more crumbling rocks until you come to a room with two small rocks and one large rock. Behind the big rock is a room with lots of ore and the Mayoi dropping a Mayoi Sign.

Contrary to what Schnabuda says, you don't have to bring him mushrooms or even fry them for the gate to open. Instead, stand in the middle of the area with the big and two small rocks in front of the room with the mayoi and jump through the ceiling. You land directly in the tower and can take care that the door opens and you can use the tower!

ALL TIPS & SOLUTIONS + GETTING STARTED TIPS

1. Uses Synthesis

You can learn the synthesis skill in the tutorial area. Especially at the beginning you quickly forget that you have it, it helps immensely and makes your weapons stronger and more durable. So experiment wildly with monster materials and Sonau parts that you attach to your weapons and shields. And don't forget the arrows! Sure, sometimes useless results come out, but you should always have a sharp weapon with you to chop down trees (a sword or an axe) and a blunt weapon so you can destroy ore deposits and cracked walls without wasting valuable Thunderflowers.

2. (Many) opponents cannot swim

Our second tip plays into the synthesis tip. If you craft a Krog Fan onto your weapon (this resource can be obtained from chopping down trees, for example), you will create gusts of wind that will blow and knock down enemies. Blow enemies into the water to get rid of them easily and without stress.

3. Throwing instead of shooting

While you can find quite a few arrows and buy supplies, once you get into the pitch-dark abyss, it's best to throw glow seeds rather than attach them to arrows. To do this, press the R button and then up on the directional pad to select the item. You make up for less distance with it, but that's tolerable.

4. Sort items

Keyword items: There are an incredible number of them in Tears of the Kingdom. Use the automatic sorting function in the menu, which you activate with the Y button. We swear by the "most used" sorting so that we don't have to scroll through the contents of the bag forever in hectic moments.

5. As above, so below

There are no shrines in the abyss, only roots that reveal the map. You must reach them and interact. Pretty difficult in the dark! But: The roots are where shrines can be found in the overworld. So if you have already found a few shrines in Hyrule, then you can orient yourself better underground and know in which direction you will find the next root. You switch between the maps with up and down on the control pad.

6. Heal miasma damage

In the Abyss, enemies covered in Miasma that hit you with an attack will lock the affected heart containers. The effect ends when you resurface, activate a root, or eat certain meals. The key to the Miasma Healing dishes is the sunspot plant. You can find them above the clouds on the sky islands, but also occasionally on the upper world, for example with fallen ruins. Use this great property of the plant to last longer in the abyss!

7. Take everything with you

In Tears of the Kingdom, your item bags are infinitely deep - well, those for weapons, shields and bows are not, but you can upgrade them with Krog seeds. What we're getting at: You can and should take whatever resources you can find with you. Not only do you always have something in your pocket for synthesis and cooking, you can always make rubies from merchants if you need the money to upgrade equipment or buy arrows. There are also some side quests that require you to hand in certain amounts of materials. Perfect if you already carry the stuff in your pocket anyway. Yes, the inventory is then all the clearer, but you are also well prepared for everything.

8. Treasures are always there for you

From time to time you meet NPCs or find treasure maps that mark places on your map where there is something to get. But you don't have to wait until that happens to find the respective treasure. Exploring is always worthwhile - the treasures are there even if nobody has told you where to find them. You should be particularly careful if you see worn, reddish flags waving in caves - they will probably lead to new armor! This also applies underground. If you recognize areas on the uncovered map that look like man-made structures, you should take a close look at them - there's bound to be something there.

9. Use gravity and stickiness

Yes, building with the Ultra Hand is fiddly at times, and yes, annoying at times. In order to align objects flat, you don't always have to twist and turn them until they fit: lift them up and turn them reasonably correctly, then drop them. Plates then usually lie flat - or at an angle, depending on how and where you drop them. And if you want to transport several things, save yourself the walking distances and simply glue everything together into a lump. You then drag it, and nothing can fall off either.

10. Use the markers

While there are only a limited number of normal markers you can place on your map, there are many other icons you can use to mark points you want to remember. We can only recommend that - Hyrule in Tears of the Kingdom is so big that you quickly lose sight of what you actually wanted to do. Organize your map so that you know, for example, where you can travel to collect certain resources, where you suspect a Krog and more.

LOCATIONS OF BIRKDA

There is a lot of content in The Legend of Zelda: Tears of the Kingdom. The Birkda saga is a type of collection and search quest. You can meet the NPC all over Hyrule. He tirelessly puts up signs for the construction company Dumsda. However, he has to support the signs all the time, otherwise they will fall over. This is where Link comes in with his Ultra Hand ability: you need to build supports out of objects lying around so Birkda can strap down the shields and move on. We have the list of places for you where you canfinds loyal assistants of Dumsda.

Birkda: Instructions

First, general tips to help Birkda - we refrain from exact solutions, not only because it's fun to tinker around, but also because there are so many ways to build supports. Most of the time - but not always - you will find a station with resources such as boards and planks in the immediate vicinity, which you can use to build scaffolding for the shield. But sometimes you have to rely on your talent for improvisation. Then grab some boulders lying around, Sonau components or simply chop down a few trees to set up supports. Also, don't forget leverage on slopes: by wedging pieces, you can give the shield support.

Birkda: Rewards

As a reward, Birkda is not only relieved and grateful, he always gives you rubies - good for your wallet. Second, he slips you rice balls. They always have different bonuses, such as endurance regeneration, heat protection and so on.

The effect depends on where you meet Birkda. The food is not only useful for satisfying Link's hunger, if you have an ingredient in the recipe - i.e. Hyrule rice - then you can see in your recipe list what you need to make the Birkda specialty yourself.

Third, you get a useful item from Birkda. You can get lodging vouchers from him for stables, thunder flowers, maniacs, and smokelings. And here is our preliminary list of Birkda's whereabouts - it is constantly being added to. If you met Birkda somewhere that we haven't listed here, please let us know in the comments and we'll add it to the list.

Where is Birkda?

- In the ruins of Hyrule City
- On the road west from the scout post

- East of Kiujoj-u Shrine, north of the road that goes around Maritta Hill and northeast of the Sorbo Plains
- Northeast of the Ebbel Forest on the beach
- On the road south of the Seres Plains leading to the Tabanta Stables. Birkda is south-southwest of the lettering on the map.
- East of the Harzblood Marshes and west of Maritta's New Stable, a lake is located on a plateau on the map. At its southern tip stands Birkda by the road.
- Cross the Tabanta Bridge from the Tabanta Stables, Birkda is directly behind
- East of Oto Bridge below Flute Grass Hill
- At the crossroads below and between Lake Aquame and Lake Komolo, where three roads meet
- Follow the path north from the Plains stable, Birkda is on the right hand side of the road at the bend
- On the hill above the shrine on the island of Melka in Ranelle Swamp
- On the road that goes north around Lake Minsh
- On the road directly at the stables on the mountain
- On the road going south past Panora Mountain
- On the Poplar Highlands southwest of the shrine by the ravine
- On the hill on the road from the plateau stable around Lake Haraja
- At the two beacons seen from the top of the Orni village
- At the Cave of Hebra Southern Point - you'll get to the area anyway if you do the story quest with Tulin of the Orni tribe
- On the south side of the Orni village on the road that goes around the lake
- In Schutar's territory just above Schutar's secret spring (the body of water to the south)
- On the road between the Snowlands Stable and Tabanta Hill
- On the road east across the Tabanta snowfield, right at the end of the Kukudja gorge
- At the end of the road in Phirone that ends in a dead end in the Nesuppo forest
- Shortly before the jetty at the stable at the lake
- East of Stall am See at the crossroads between Angelstedt and Lockfrit-Berg
- At the end of the road towards the Institute from the East Akkala Stables

- In East Necluda, north-east of the tower in the Labella Marshes in the pass between Mount Hime-Ida and the Zukaje Plateau
- In Necluda on the plain between Quorta Highlands and Folbluth Plains at the entrance to the west gate of Ranelle Road
- South of the East Akkala stable between the two roads leading south
- Between West Necluda and East Necluda in the Esch Marsh east of the Twin Mountains stable
- Head north from Maritta's new stables, just after the two roads merge

If you ever want to meet Birkda's boss, Dumsda, then you should head northeast. In Akkala is the settlement of Taburasa, where you will meet the builder. You can also build a house here!

SAGONO QUEST - FIND EIGHT NPCS

You probably know the village of Hateno from The Legend of Zelda: Breath of the Wild. In The Legend of Zelda: Tears of the Kingdom, things are smoldering in what is actually a quiet place: star designer Sagono and the incumbent mayor Rietnar are at loggerheads. Vegetables or fashion, what should Hateno focus on? You are part of the dispute and are obligated by Sagono to give a Hyrule Mushroom to eight NPCs in the village in order to convince them of her as a candidate for the mayoral post of Hateno.

Who to give Hyrule Mushrooms to?

Sagono is very precise about which eight residents of Hateno you should give a mushroom: no people who already support Sagono, no children and no newcomers - like the teacher at school. Luckily, you can recognize the people from the anti-Sagono faction by their "unfashionable" clothing. Anyone who wears a mushroom hat or even an entire ensemble of Sagono clothes falls out of the list.

However, it is not that easy to find all Hateno NPCS that fit this description, since they all have a day-to-day business. Here is our list of people and where to find them.

Sagono or Rietnar?

- **Watargo**, the husband of the owner of the inn, is skeptical about Sagono. He can be found on the balcony of the building or inside.
- **Meddo**is the tomato farmer who tends his vegetables behind the house most of the time. If you enter Hateno from the street, you will find him on the left.
- **Tamana**You can meet her in the yard of her house, also to the left of Hateno's entrance, where she takes care of the chickens. In the evening she sweeps the path at the entrance to the village.
- Just below the school is a field tended by old lady Ume. She stays there all day.
- **Farvel**you will find in the evening in the inn in the dining room while eating
- You will find the last three at the top of the farm, above all Farmer Dodanz, who takes care of the cows all day long. By the way, you can exchange three acorns for a bottle of fresh milk with him - practical!
- Farmer Koyin is either in the pasture or in the house if you have already completed her quest with the message in a bottle in the pond.
- The final Sagono Defiant is Tokk. Early in the morning he sits by the cooking fire in front of the farm, then he climbs the path up to the Hateno Institute.

So you get rid of all eight mushrooms and Sagono is pleased with Link's use. But that's not the end of the mayoral dispute between Sagono and Rietnar - they both have a few secrets... but you can find out for yourself.

FIND BAUTOMATIC - THE GUIDE

Link's new arm in The Legend of Zelda: Tears of the Kingdom is a real marvel: thanks to it, the long-eared hero can jump through ceilings, stick objects together and even turn back time. By the time you've exited the Forgotten Skyislands tutorial section, Link has mastered most of the important skills. But you've probably noticed that there's still an empty slot in the ring menu. That's where the Bautomatik belongs! We have recorded for you how and where you can get them.

This is how the automatic works

It pays to get the Bautomatik as early as possible. Because with it you can easily recreate everything you have already built with the Ultra Hand with just the push of a button! This even works if you don't have the required parts with you. Anything missing will be replaced with Sonanium from your inventory. You can find the rare metal in the abyss under Hyrule. You also have to go there to get the Bautomatik. In the abyss you will also meet friendly constructs again and again at abandoned mines, which will give you new blueprints, for example for airplanes or vehicles. And in the hiding places of the Yiga-Band there are also boards to get, which give you practical blueprints for the Bautomatik.

Locality Bautomatik

You can reach the Hyrule Abyss by jumping through the red holes in the overworld. The quickest route to the Bautomatic is via Mount Hylia. It's on the Forgotten Plateau - you might remember it as the starting area in Zelda: Breath of the Wild. On the Forgotten Plateau, continue up Hylia Mountain to the small pond next to which you can see a chasm marked in red. You must jump into this abyss - be careful not to touch the miasma-covered walls.

There is an elevator at the bottom. Take him and you come to carts and rails. Use the cart on the left, the rails on the right are cut. Drive down the stations until you get to the Abandoned Central Mine. Here you are right for the Bautomatik! Ride or jump further up and pray at the giant statue. Then go up the stairs opposite and jump further up from there. You see two "researchers" and a construct. The construct gives you the Bautomatik. In addition, she gets to the bottom of the nasty Yiga gang.

www.ingramcontent.com/pod-product-compliance
Lightning Source LLC
LaVergne TN
LVHW081346050326
832903LV00024B/1354